THE QUILTER'S

*Night Before Christmas*

# THE QUILTER'S
# *Night Before Christmas*
## A TREASURY OF TRADITION

*Sue Reich*

SCHIFFER PUBLISHING

4880 Lower Valley Road • Atglen, PA 19310

Designed by Ashley Millhouse
Cover design by Ashley Millhouse
Type set in Canto Pen/Baskerville

ISBN: 978-0-7643-6243-9
Printed in China

Published by Schiffer Publishing, Ltd.
4880 Lower Valley Road
Atglen, PA 19310
Phone: (610) 593-1777; Fax: (610) 593-2002
E-mail: Info@schifferbooks.com
Web: www.schifferbooks.com

For our complete selection of fine books on this and related subjects, please visit our website at www.schifferbooks.com. You may also write for a free catalog.

Schiffer Publishing's titles are available at special discounts for bulk purchases for sales promotions or premiums. Special editions, including personalized covers, corporate imprints, and excerpts, can be created in large quantities for special needs. For more information, contact the publisher.

We are always looking for people to write books on new and related subjects. If you have an idea for a book, please contact us at proposals@ schifferbooks.com.

Page 2: Quilt by Susan Fiondella, Vero Beach, Florida. Cotton, machine pieced, machine embroidered, machine quilted.

**Other Schiffer Books by the Author:**

*World War II Quilts, 2nd Edition*, ISBN 978-0-7643-5334-5

*Quilts Presidential and Patriotic*, ISBN 978-0-7643-5041-2

*Quiltings, Frolicks, & Bees*, ISBN 978-0-7643-4098-7

Clement Clark Moore, *The Night Before Christmas* (New York, London, and Paris: Raphael Tuck & Sons, 1901), page 3

Ellen K. Clapsaddle, 1906

*Dedicated to those who are*
*forever young at heart and*
*keeping quilts in Christmas.*

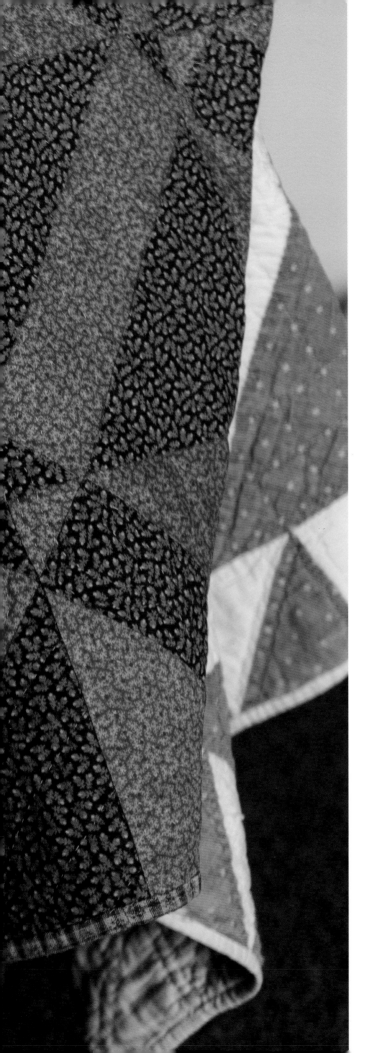

# Contents

# INTRODUCTION

My strong German heritage is most likely responsible for our family's love of Christmas. Each year, we celebrate the holiday with all the trimmings—candlelights in each window, cookie baking, gingerbread houses, wreaths, red bows and roping, a Christmas tree with vintage and personalized ornaments, an antique quilt tree skirt, and family gatherings. In the 1990s, as my firstborn child left for Europe and his career in the military, I vowed to cover each bed in our home with a red-and-green festive quilt for our next family Christmas back in Connecticut. That was the beginning of my Christmas quiltmaking. Over the years, I've come to realize that quilts and Christmas are the perfect blend: both represent expressions of true love for your family. Both add beauty, comfort, a festive spirit, and happiness within your home. Even back thirty years ago, one of my holiday activities became "keeping quilts in Christmas."

It was a trip to Colonial Williamsburg and viewing an exhibit about Clement C. Moore and his famous "'Twas the Night Before Christmas" poem that inspired this book. In 2015, the Abby Aldrich Rockefeller Folk Art Museum featured an exhibit recognizing Dr. Moore and the holiday poem he penned in 1822, almost two hundred years ago. As a quilt historian who loves to memorialize important historical marker dates, the idea of making quilts to showcase the most famous Christmas poem and featuring them in a book and exhibit seemed a great way to commemorate the anniversary.

TOP LEFT: Sampler Christmas stars, hand pieced, hand quilted, cotton, 79 × 79 inches. My first Christmas quilt was made in 1998 during the holiday season. I designed the blocks using star quilt blocks featured in Barbara Brackman's *Encyclopedia of Pieced Quilt Patterns* (1993), with festive novelty prints of the '90s. My challenge was to use only the fabrics within my stash.

BOTTOM LEFT: *Must Be Santa*, machine pieced, hand appliquéd, machine quilted, cotton, 54 × 79 inches. Probably our favorite Christmas quilt; I designed this quilt to highlight '90s fabric featuring Santa as the star. One of my children's favorite Christmas songs from the Mitch Miller sing-along album *Must Be Santa*. All told, I've made about a dozen Christmas quilts for my family.

It was in December 1822 when Dr. Clement C. Moore penned his immortal poem "A Visit from St. Nicholas." His intention was to present a gift of a holiday poem to his five young children. Two hundred years later, ten generations of children have fantasized about a jolly, old elf arriving with goodies each Christmas Eve. Parents continue to carry forth the tradition of reading what is now known as" 'Twas the Night Before Christmas."

Clement Clark Moore, *Night Before Christmas (*Newark, NJ, and New York: Charles E. Graham, 1910), page 1

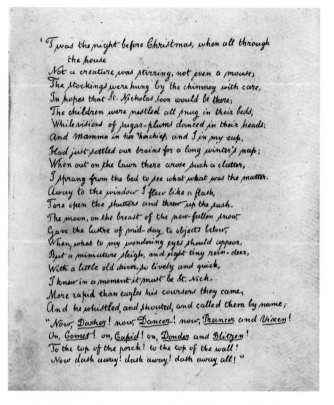

One of only four copies of *A Visit from St. Nicholas* penned by Dr. Clement C. Moore. New York Historical Society, public domain.

Real Photo postcard, Lipp Studios, Philadelphia

Clement Clarke Moore, engraved by J. W. Evans

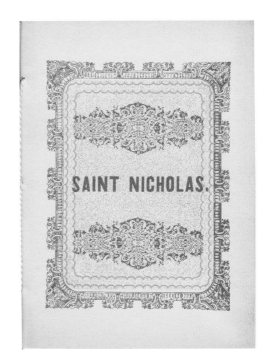

Facsimile of an 1849 version of *A Visit from St. Nicholas*

Clement C. Moore was born into a wealthy New York City family. His father was an Episcopal bishop and the president of Columbia College. His mother, Charity Clarke, was the daughter of a retired British officer who purchased a piece of land on Manhattan Island extending from Eighth Avenue to the Hudson River. Clement inherited the mansion built on the property, named "Chelsea," and donated much of the remaining land for the construction of an Episcopalian theological seminary. Dr. Moore served as a faculty member at the seminary, holding a position until his death at age eighty-three on July 10, 1863.[1]

During the 1822 holiday season, the Moore family hosted the family of Dr. David Butler of St. Paul's Church, Troy, New York. Dr. Butler's eldest daughter requested and received permission to copy "A Visit from St. Nicholas" in her album. The following year, the poem was published on the third page of the *Troy Sentinel*.[2] Each year after, the poem was published without attribution to the author. In 1824, the *New York Spectator* published the following account accompanying the poem:

We know not to whom we are indebted for the following description of that unwearied patron of

children—that homely, but delightful personification of parental kindness, Sainte Claus, his costume and his equipage, as he goes about visiting the fire-sides of this happy land, laden with Christmas bounties; but, from whomsoever it may have come, we give thanks for it. There is, to our apprehension, a spirit of cordial goodness in it, a playfulness of fancy, and a benevoalacrity to enter into the feeling and promote the simple pleasures of children, which are altogether charming. We hope our little patrons, both lads and lasses, will accept it as proof of our unfeigned good will towards them—as a token of our warmest wish that they may have many a merry Christmas; that they may long retain their beautiful relish for those unbought, homebred joys, which derive their flavor from filial piety and fraternal love, and which they may be assured are the least alloyed that time can furnish them; and that they may never part with that simplicity of character, which is their own fairest ornament, and for the sake of which they have been pronounced, by authority which none can say, the types of such as shall inherit the Kingdom of God.[3]

1   "The Man Who Wrote 'The Night Before Christmas.'" *Daily Register Gazette*, Thursday, December 12, 1912, page 16.
2   Joseph Jackson in *World's Work*, "The Night Before Christmas," republished in *Arizona Republican*, Thursday, December 26, 1912, page 5.
3   *New York Spectator*, Thursday, January 1, 1824, page 1.

ST. NICK AND HIS TEAM.

Earliest image of St. Nick to accompany "The Night Before Christmas" poem, *Saturday Courier* (Philadelphia), December 25, 1847, page 2

A Visit from Santa Claus.

BY CLEMENT C. MOORE.

Civil War–era image of St. Nicholas from the *Western Reserve Chronicle* (Warren, OH), December 26, 1866, page 2

v.

"A Visit from Saint Nicholas."

By Clement C. Moore.

" Twas the night before Christmas, and all through the house
Not a creature was stirring, not even a mouse."

Illustrated in Tints, from Drawings by F. O. C. Darley.

This is a very elegant edition of the above famous Christmas Poem. It is printed in style and size similar to our editions of the "Star Spangled Banner," "Flag," etc., with an exquisitely illuminated cover, and colored title-page. It will be a popular Christmas trifle. (Nearly Ready.)

Price Fifty Cents.

Early add for an illustrated *A Visit for Saint Nicholas* published in the *Boston Traveler*, December 4, 1862, page 3

In 1844, the author of "A Visit from St. Nicholas" finally claimed authorship, when the poem and other written works of Dr. Moore were published. One of the first illustrated versions was printed around 1849–50. In 1862, the entire epic poem was illustrated by acclaimed illustrator F. O. C. Darley. Reaching immediate popularity, it was included in grade-school readers nationwide.[4] A preamble to the poem at the beginning of the Civil War era in an 1861 *Hartford Daily Courant* read:

> The following, from the pen of Prof. Moore, has been in print a long time; but it wears well, and we think some of our young readers may like to see it. The troubles of war are transient; but the great fact on which Christianity is based, is as fixed as the everlasting hills.[5]

After the Civil War, the introduction to the famous poem read:

> No record of Christmas would be complete without the admirable production of Clement C. Moore, which, to old heads, recalls the happy days of childhood, and to the little folks is a never-failing source of wonder. Though familiar to the majority of readers, we append it as a standard Christmas poem which never wears out, but which will be the delight of the children as long as our language is read.[6]

> We publish this morning, for the benefit of all of our young readers, those beautiful lines descriptive of Santa Claus' visit the bedside of the sleeping children—written by Prof. Moore. We know the little ones will be glad to hear them read, for it tells them how the benevolent old Saint comes so well prepared to fill their stockings with toys and good things.
> And here we may be allowed to expressed the hope that all the dear children in Charlestown, may awake Christmas morning to find their brightest anticipations realized.[7]

The popularity of this Christmas poem increased during the last half of the nineteenth century, through the twentieth, and now into the twenty-first century. On each Christmas Eve, generation after generation makes it their family tradition to have a reading of "Twas the Night Before Christmas." A gift originally meant only for the Moore children has delighted ten generations of youth, sending them off to their beds as visions of sugar plums dance in their heads.

---

4    Joseph Jackson in *World's Work*, "The Night Before Christmas," republished in *Arizona Republican*, Thursday, December 26, 1912, page 5.

5    "Christmas," *Hartford Daily Courant*, Wednesday, December 25, 1861, page 2.

6    "Christmas Eve," *St. Paul Dispatch*, Thursday, December 24, 1868, page 2.

7    "The Night Before Christmas," *Spirit of Jefferson* (Charles Town, West Virginia), Tuesday, December 20, 1870, page 4.

Image of St. Nicholas from the 1849 facsimile of *A Visit from St. Nicholas*

*Denslow's Night Before Christmas* (Chicago: M. A. Donohue, 1902)

*The Night Before Christmas*, illustrations by Margaret Evans Price (Rochester, NY: Stecher Litho., 1917)

A multitude of renditions of the Noel visit frequently feature quilts from the earliest illustrations, particularly in the third stanza:

> The children were nestled all snug in their beds,
>
> While visions of sugar-plums danced in their heads.

Quilts as bedcoverings have been featured in "'Twas the Night Before Christmas" for over 150 years. Many of these images were also the inspiration for this book: combining quilts and Christmas. The patterns and styles of the quilts reflect the popular quiltmaking trends at the time of each publication.

To keep quilts in Christmas and to honor the two hundredth commemorative year of Dr. Clement C. Moore's poem, I challenged my quilt-making friends, many of whom are quilt historians, to pick a stanza and re-create their memories of reading this famous childhood poem. Each maker chose a favorite stanza to be represented in a quilt. The criteria were simple:

- Create a quilt, sized 24 × 30 inches in a vertical setting, to represent your stanza (do not include your stanza on the quilt).
- It can be inspired by an antique book, postcard, card, coloring book, etc.
- Must include a miniature quilt or quilted image somewhere in the quilt.
- Place a 4 inch sleeve on the back with a label.
- Avoid embellishments that extend far off the quilt surface.
- No photo transfers, with the exception of faces, if desired.
- Reads in shades of red, green, and white, with other accent colors.

*Denslow's Night Before Christmas* (Chicago: M. A. Donahue & Co., 1902)

I am most grateful to the following people:

Susan Fiondella, who created the small stanza quilts specifically for this project. The stanza quilts will accompany this book, *The Quilter's Night Before Christmas*, as it travels the nation on exhibit.

Ann Parsons Holte, who provided her talent and precise patterning for the antique and newly designed nine reindeer quilts.

Barb Garrett and Ann Parsons Holte, who provided their expertise and muscle with quilt photography.

My editors Sandra Korinchak and Helena Neufeld and the staff of Schiffer Publishing, who provided enthusiasm and support in commemorating the two hundredth anniversary of "'Twas the Night Before Christmas."

# "A VISIT FROM SAINT NICHOLAS"
# IN QUILTS

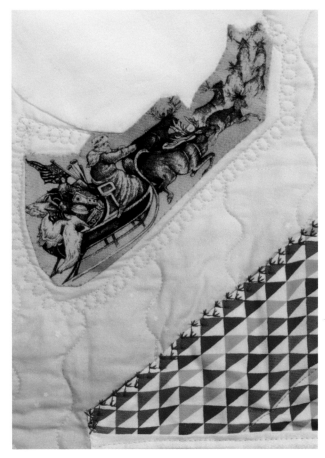

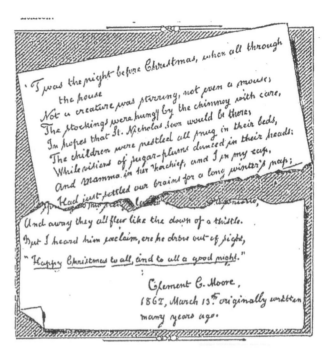

'Twas the night-before Christmas, when all through the house
Not a creature was stirring, not even a mouse;
The stockings were hung by the chimney with care,
In hopes that St. Nicholas soon would be there;
The children were nestled all snug in their beds,
While visions of sugar-plums danced in their heads;
And mamma in her kerchief, and I in my cap,
Had just settled our brains for a long winter's nap;

And away they all flew like the down of a thistle.
But I heard him exclaim, ere he drove out of sight,
"Happy Christmas to all, and to all a good night."

Clement C. Moore,
1862, March 13th originally written
many years ago.

Sue Reich, Washington Depot, Connecticut

Cotton, machine and hand appliquéd, hand embroidery

My inspiration for the title quilt for this exhibit is a cozy living room on Christmas Eve all set for the arrival of Santa Claus. The nutcrackers are a shout-out to my German heritage. The eagle fireback expresses our family's patriotic spirit. During the holidays, I spend the two weeks before Christmas baking cookies. Cookie platters are my edible gifts of love to family and friends. No matter the age of our children or grandchildren, Santa is still offered a plate of cookies on Christmas Eve. The five stockings hanging on the mantle are fragments of antique quilts and represent me, my husband, and our three children. Miniature quilts can be found as the Christmas tree skirt and the star quilt over the fireplace.

Marjorie Farquharson, Needham, Massachusetts | Quilted by Vickie Murchison Maloney

Cotton, hand appliquéd, machine pieced, hand embroidered, machine quilted

Clement Clarke Moore lived at Chelsea, his family estate in New York City, when he penned his famous Christmas poem. Mary C. Moore Ogden sketched his home for the first published color edition of the work. I used her sketch of the house as my inspiration for the opening stanza. I took the liberty of including Christmas ornaments even though they wouldn't be introduced as a Christmas tradition until later in the nineteenth century. And, of course, there is a little mouse.

LEFT: *Chelsea Mansion*, by Mary C. Ogden (daughter of Clement C. Moore), cropped by Beyond My Ken (*talk*), 01:39, June 28, 2010. UTC / public domain.

RIGHT: *Denslow's Night Before Christmas*, illustrations by W. W. Denslow (Chicago: M. A. Donohue, 1902)

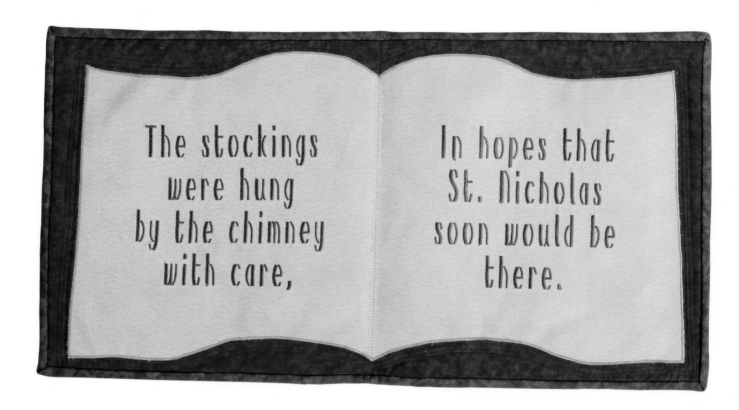

The stockings were hung by the chimney with care,

In hopes that St. Nicholas soon would be there.

Teddy Pruett, Lake City, Florida

Cotton, machine pieced and machine appliquéd, beading, star and vintage embellishments, fragments of vintage quilts, machine quilted

This poem usually conjures images of a Victorian Christmas, but I wanted to portray a cabin Christmas. Simple, basic, but still filled with love, joy, and anticipation. This was meant to be a southern US cabin, but it could be anywhere.

*St. Nicholas and Little Snowdrop*, unknown origin

Susan Fiondella, Vero Beach, Florida

Cotton, machine pieced, machine embroidered, machine quilted

Inspired by children everywhere, I chose this stanza of the poem to create my quilt. There is nothing more exciting for a child on Christmas Eve than going to bed anticipating the next morning's celebration. Excitement abounds. Each one dreams their dreams. We live in a different era than that of the poem, but children everywhere still love Christmas and dream. It was the same for me and my four sisters, and it is the same for my two grandchildren depicted in my pictorial of this timeless poem.

Since I have always loved this poem, I enjoyed working on this project and stretching my sewing and artistic skills. Fond memories of Christmases past fill my heart with joy. Christmas blessings to you all!

RIGHT: *The Night Before Christmas Animated,* illustrations and animations by Julian Wehr (New York: Duenewald, 1949)

LEFT: *The Night Before Christmas,* illustrations by Fern Bisel Peat (Akron, OH: Saalfield, 1936)

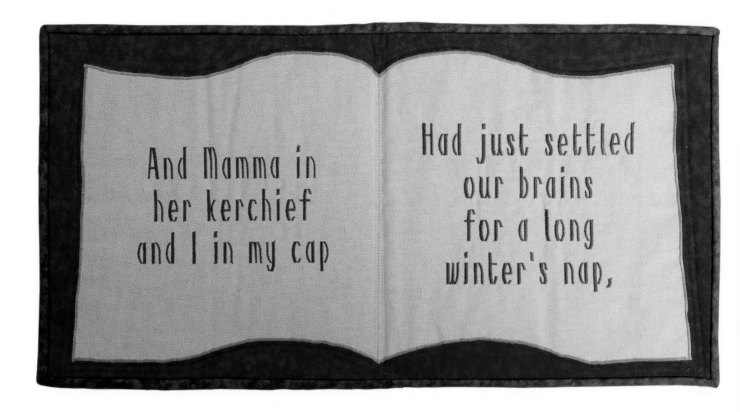

Lisa Erlandson, Gainesville, Texas

Cotton, machine pieced and machine appliquéd, hand embroidered, metallic threads, machine quilted

*Denslow's Night Before Christma*s, illustrations by W. W. Denslow (Chicago: M. A. Donohue, 1902)

I have known the poem "A Visit from St. Nicholas" (""Twas the Night Before Christmas") as long as I can remember! I still have the book that I was given as a very young child, and have enjoyed sharing it with my children and grandchildren through the years.

The stanza above certainly has more meaning to me as an adult than it did as a child. Preparing for that visit from Santa and for the festivities to come on Christmas Day definitely makes one wish for a long winter's nap.

When I envisioned this quilt, I wanted to portray a setting that could have been seen in 1822, when this poem was written, so I researched the bed styles and even the type of gas lamp (an Argand lamp) that might been used two hundred years ago. The Candlewick bed covering would have also been typical of the time period. The narrator of the poem and "Momma" are settling their brains in an early 1820s bedroom.

I also envisioned what my idea of a "long winter's nap" would look like. I love the stars in the winter sky. They seem brighter and sparkle more clearly on a cold winter night. Many people describe a sky such as this to be covered with a blanket of stars, but of course we all know that it is really a quilt of stars! The sawtooth star would have been a quilt pattern in use two hundred years ago, but I added twenty-first-century-style fabrics to make the stars shine. The larger star is my interpretation of the Christmas star, using the pattern Star of the East. As a child, I remember searching the night sky on Christmas Eve looking for Santa and wondering which bright star was the Christmas star that the Wise Men had seen and followed.

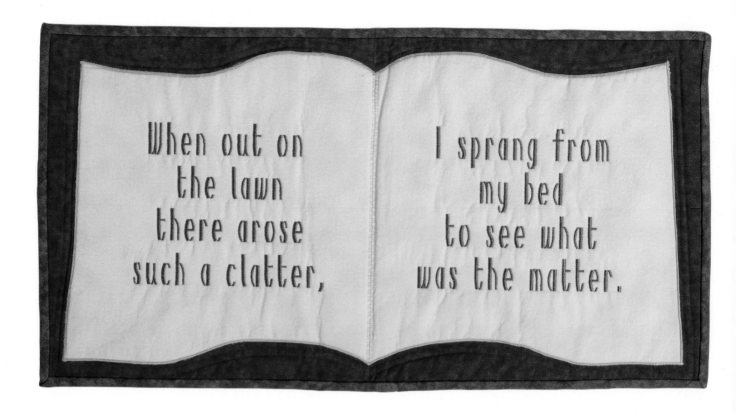

Marsha Regan, Rochester, New York

Cotton, machine pieced and raw-edge appliqué, machine quilted

I have been quilting for over thirty years, and this was my first art quilt. It was a very challenging project, and I realized that I am my own worst enemy when it comes to working outside my comfort zone. This was a fun experience to capture the excitement and wonder of the clatter arising on Christmas Eve.

*The Night Before Christmas*, drawings by Margaret Evans Price
(Rochester, NY: Stecher Litho., 1917)

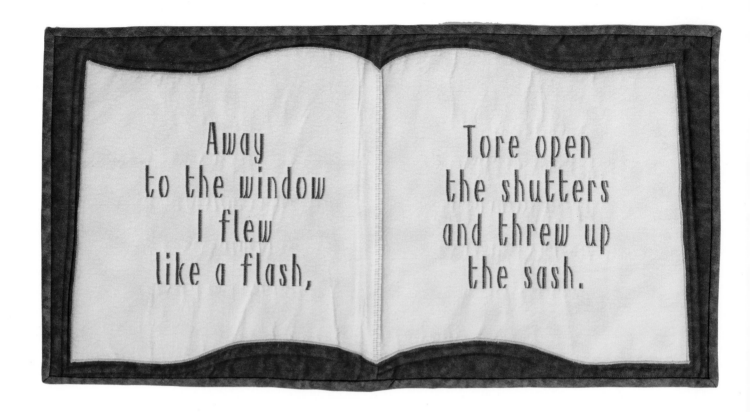

Away
to the window
I flew
like a flash,

Tore open
the shutters
and threw up
the sash.

Carol Poitras, Newmarket, New Hampshire

Cotton, machine pieced, hand appliquéd, vintage embellishments, machine quilted

I have always loved "The Night Before Christmas" by Clement Moore. Although my children are all grown, I still read the book every Christmas Eve. In fact, long ago, I added the words "Now go to bed!" to the end of the book, which makes everyone laugh as each of them goes off to their rooms for that long winter's nap.

I completed this project with my fabric stash and did not buy a thing. The crocheted curtain pull and the decoration on the quilted shade were made by my grandmother Mary Ann (May) Moore, born in 1885. As a child, I often wondered if Clement Moore was a long-lost relative. I am still hunting for that information.

I enjoyed creating the design and seeing it come to life: even those needle-turn appliquéd hands.

*The Night Before Christmas*, illustrations by Fern Bisel Peat (Akron, OH: Saalfield, 1936)

Sharon Waddell, New Windsor, New York

Cotton, machine pieced, machine appliquéd, button and paint embellishments, machine quilted

I wanted to portray the stillness of the night, so I kept the scene very simple. Looking down out the window, you see nothing but a quilt hanging on the line with the full moon rising. The little quilt is pieced, its shadow a mixture of fabric paints. The stars are both fabric paint and thread.

*The Night Before Christmas*, illustrations by Cornelius DeWitt (New York: Simon & Schuster, 1946)

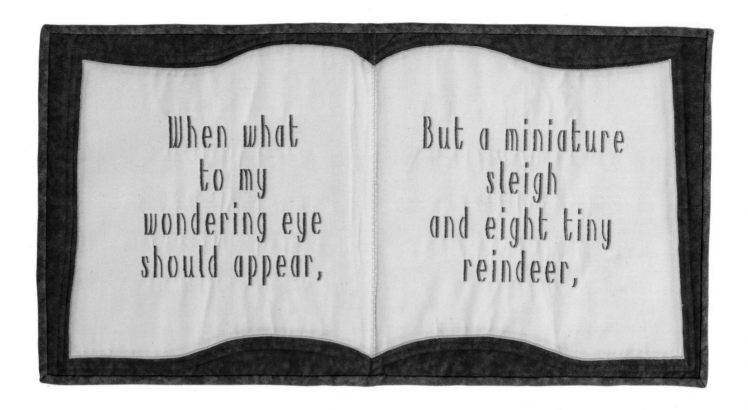

Madge Ziegler, Newark, Delaware

Cotton and wool; machine pieced; hand appliquéd; hand embroidered; embellished with metallic threads, sequins, stars, and beads; hand and machine quilted

With a collection of copies of "The Night Before Christmas" spanning almost fifty years, I had about forty-five books to consult. Narrowing it down to five copies, I combined ideas for this piece—small sketches; a full-size draft on graph paper followed.

Many hours were spent trying to create a sense of perspective, choosing woodwork fabrics, and portraying a face. I chose a well-felted wool sweater (ruined by aggressive washing many years ago) to create the robe, and I cut down a Christmas log cabin table runner to make the valance.

Pictorial quilts are not my specialty, so this one was a real challenge. I had to give up the idea of it being perfect, and settle for "Can you tell what this is supposed to be?"

*The Night Before Christmas*, illustrations by William Smedley, Frederic B. Schell, Alfred Fredericks, and Henry R. Poore (Philadelphia: Porter & Coates, 1883)

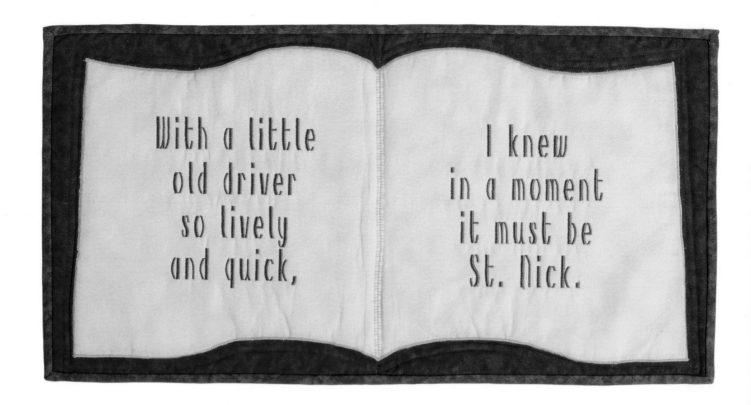

With a little
old driver
so lively
and quick,

I knew
in a moment
it must be
St. Nick.

Sue Reich, Washington Depot, Connecticut

Cotton, hand and machine appliquéd, machine quilted

My design was inspired by outline images of St. Nick. I enlarged the lines and machine appliquéd Santa as one piece in its entirety to the background fabrics. This was my first attempt at such an intricate large piece of fabric. Fragments of antique quilts to represent mini bell quilts and the quilted ball of St. Nick's cap fulfill the requirements of the Christmas challenge to include miniature quilts in the design.

*The Night Before Christmas*, illustrations by Fern Bisel Peat (Akron, OH: Saalfield, 1936)

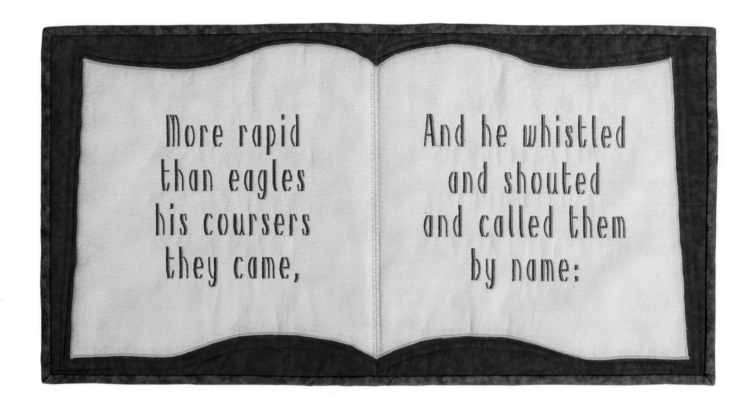

More rapid
than eagles
his coursers
they came,

And he whistled
and shouted
and called them
by name:

Jill Meszaros, Cambridge Springs, Pennsylvania

Cotton, hand appliquéd, hand embroidered, hand quilted

Snowy farm scenes are familiar in bucolic Crawford County, Pennsylvania, where I call home. With proximity to Lake Erie, the county also receives its share of lake effect snow. My quilt captures the popularity of barn quilts. During the past two decades, quilt blocks have been painted on the sides of barns. The star quilt block replicates one painted on my barn welcoming Santa on Christmas Eve. I call this quilt "My little farm in the hills of PA."

Living on our farm in northwestern Pennsylvania, I see eagles almost daily. Those eagles are what inspired me to create this scene in my quilt. This is how I have always envisioned Santa as he flies overhead our farm on Christmas Eve.

*The Night Before Christmas,* drawings by Margaret Evans Price (Rochester, NY: Stecher Litho., 1917)

"Now, Dasher! Now, Dancer! Now, Prancer and Vixen!

On Comet! On Cupid! On Donder and Blitzen!

Sandra Starley, Fillmore, Utah

Cotton, machine and paper piecing, hand appliquéd, hand embroidered, metallic threads, machine quilted

The original design was inspired by Santa's famous team. When I saw the call, I immediately thought of this stanza, since I'd designed an appliqué reindeer block years ago and knew that it would make a great reindeer crew. I created a pyramid of reindeer, playing on the language that seems to depict a stack of reindeer standing on top of each other (on Comet, on Cupid, on Donner). I decided to make each reindeer out of a different brown fabric to add interest. I made a custom saddle blanket for each reindeer, using different fabric and patterns for each. It was so fun to find the perfect "reindeer names" fabrics in my sister Donna's stash—just the right size to fussy-cut and ID the team members on their quilted blankets. I used metallic embroidery thread for their halters and lead lines to add sparkle. I found a Christmas holly fabric in my mom Georgia's stash for the border (it takes a village). It was a small piece, so I added a Santa print and gave him to the reins/line. My favorite wonky-paper-pieced stars completed the border. A retro Christmas print from our stash made a fun back, and finally, a delightful printed plaid binding was found on a birthday shopping trip. The quilting is very textural in the main section, with all the outlining and stars, while the border stars are more subtle. Making the quilt was definitely an interesting journey, since I experimented and created as I went. I hope it makes you smile. Follow the lead line from Santa to Blitzen to read the stanza in order.

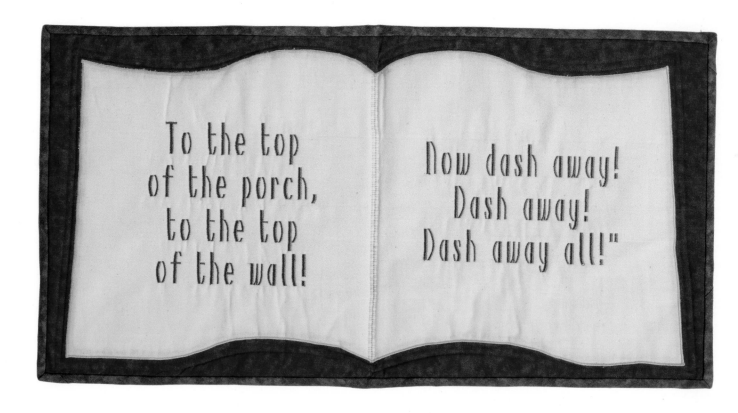

Doris Bloomer, Augusta, Georgia

Cotton, hand and machine pieced and quilted

"'Twas the Night Before Christmas" is one of my daughter-in-law's favorite poems. Christmas wouldn't be complete without it being read multiple times during the Christmas season. I was thrilled to get chosen to make a quilt for the exhibit and to receive stanza 12. Right away, I pictured Santa flying with his sleigh past the house and up the porch. I wanted to make the house out of Log Cabin blocks with a good-sized front porch, nice and old fashioned, with rolling snowy hills. The dark sky, the twinkling stars . . . and when I found the perfect fabric for the sky I was all set! I mostly machine quilted the quilt—however, I wanted to add some hand quilting to the project, as that is really my favorite way of finishing a quilt top.

Postcard, "Whitney Made," Worcester, MA, 1918

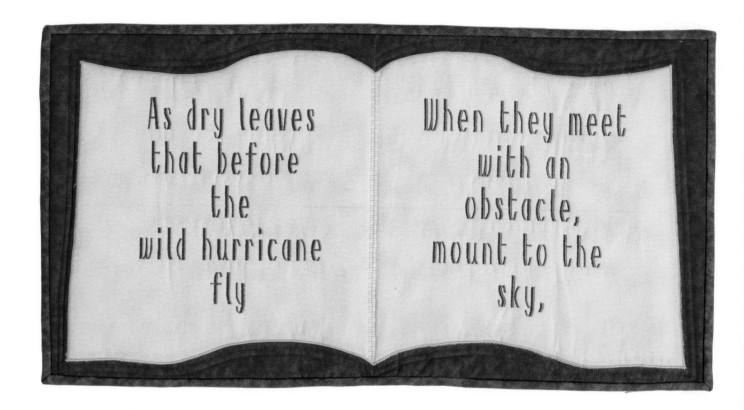

Sue Reich, Washington Depot, Connecticut

Cotton and cork, machine pieced and machine appliquéd, hand penciled, machine quilted

The woods surrounding our home on a snowy December's night in the foothills of the Berkshires and the mice who camp outside awaiting the arrival of St. Nick were the inspiration for my quilt. A little mouse snoozes away, all comfy cozy, in his walnut shell, wrapped in his miniature, gray, patchwork quilt. Dry leaves fussy-cut from a flannel print represent the dry leaves from our pin oak, flying up in a swirl. The Christmas trees are antique quilt fragments. All in all, my goal was to depict a quiet, peaceful Christmasy scene.

*The Night Before Christmas*, illustrations by Cornelius DeWitt (New York: Simon & Schuster, 1946). The inspiration for this stanza.

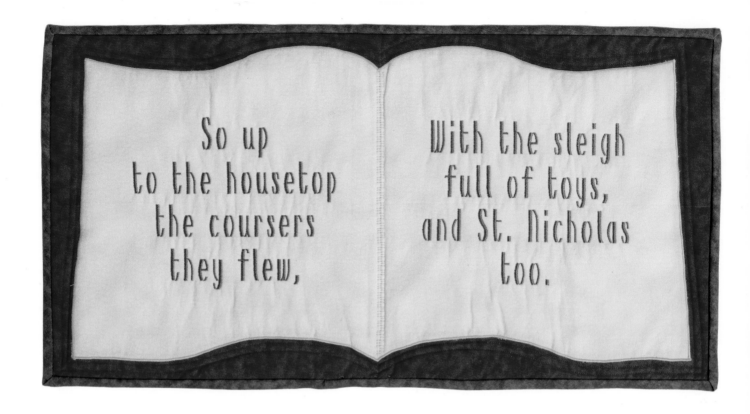

So up
to the housetop
the coursers
they flew,

With the sleigh
full of toys,
and St. Nicholas
too.

Sue Reich, Washington Depot, Connecticut

Cotton, hand and machine appliqued, metallic cording, machine quilting.

The inspiration for this quilt was my home on Christmas Eve. We live in the Litchfield Hills of Connecticut surrounded by pine trees. My house is made of stone quarried on our property, a wreath always decorates our door at Christmas. I used fragments of an antique quilt cut into Christmas trees to further decorate the scene. The miniature red and green quilt is featured on Santa's sleigh filled with toys as he flies off to his next destination.

Postcard, "Whitney Made," Worcester, MA, 1918

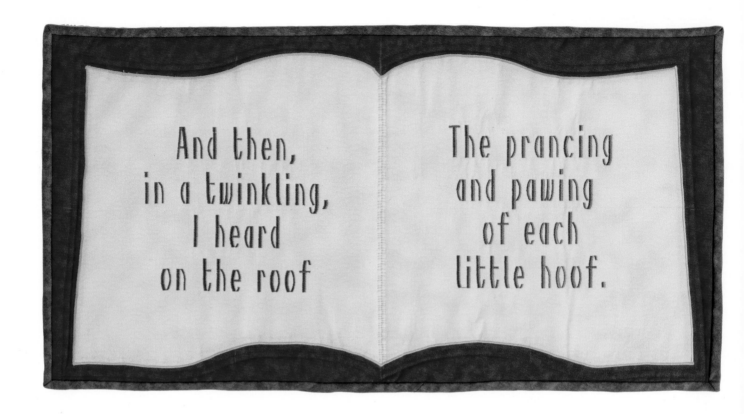

Jayne Steffens, Racine, Wisconsin

Cotton, machine pieced and machine appliquéd, machine quilted, metallic thread embellishment

The verse of the "The Night Before Christmas" seemed to call for an audio interpretation. So the challenge for me was to see the sound. Yikes! Visions of eight reindeer and all thirty-two hoofs danced in my head but refused to take shape on cloth, so I settled with depicting only dancing hoofs. Dancers seem to like glitz, so I had to include a little metallic thread. I hope the viewers of this piece can "hear" those reindeer!

Postcard, "Whitney Made," Worcester, MA, 1918

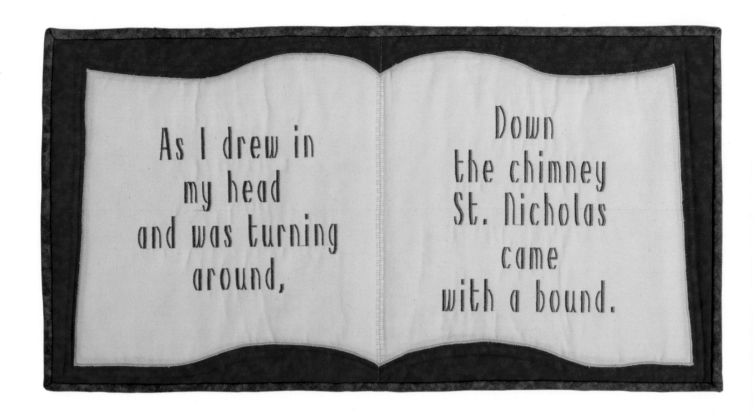

Kathy Cray, Ormond Beach, Florida | Quilted by Vicki Murchison Maloney

Cotton, machine pieced and machine appliquéd, embellished with cording, machine quilted

My quilt was inspired by my childhood memories and my intrigue of "who" actually was Santa Claus. Above the fireplace is a photo of my sister and me sitting on Santa's lap; little did we know at the time that Santa was our dad! For years after that photo was taken, I would seek out the Christmas presents I believed to be stashed in our home. Some years I found them, and other times I was not as lucky.

American Postcard "Christmas" series, #1713 (New York: Ullman, 1929)

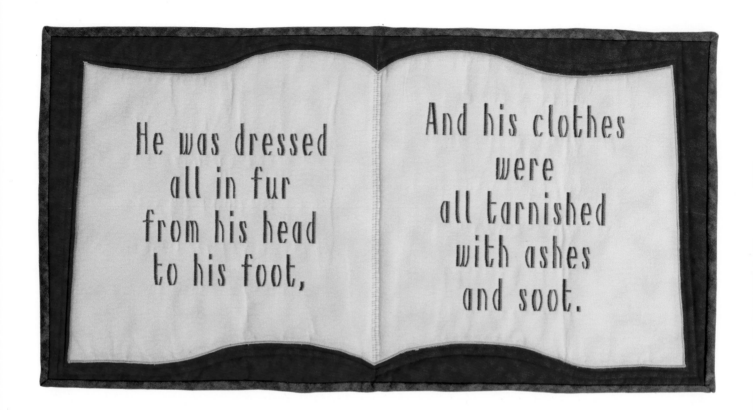

Sara Reimer Farley, Wichita Kansas, Quilted by Kim Hull, Andover, Kansas

Cotton, hand and machine pieced, prismacolor pencils, machine quilted.

My inspiration came from two sources, the traditional Chimney Sweep block and my collection of St. Nicholas figures. My favorite St. Nicks have long robes in the European tradition perhaps because of a belief in a St. Nick clad in such a robe and riding a white horse endured longer than the magic of Santa Claus for my younger son. So my St. Nick has a long red robe, trimmed in sooty fur, of course, from sweeping down the chimney.

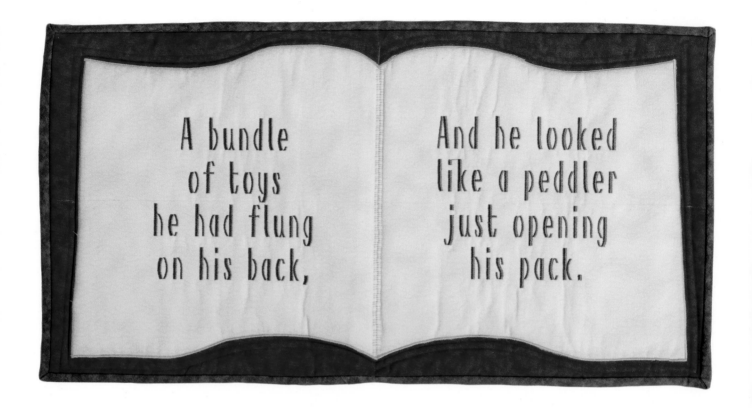

Karen Alexander, Lopez Island, Washington

Cotton, hand appliquéd, hand embroidered, embellished with metallic threads and dimensional draperies, hand quilted

What a walk down memory lane this project has been. A child's world of fantasy and make-believe is so magical and powerful, perhaps especially so at Christmastime. This quilt definitely has lots of stories within it for me.

My main inspiration came from an image I found online from a circa 1900 child's book. I viewed many iconic Santa scenes online and integrated bits and pieces of ideas from several sources into my final design, experimenting and improvising with fabrics as I went along. I think that is what I enjoyed the most about the process . . . the "improve" as ideas popped up. I even squealed with delight when I found the fabric of Mrs. Claus stitching away on a quilt from my mother-in-law Wini's stash, perfect for the creation of a "thought bubble," as though coming from Santa's thoughts.

The musical notes on the stocking fabric, as well as the musical instruments under the tree and in Santa's pack, are a salute to my husband. We met through our mutual love of choral music while in college, and it has been a huge part of our lives ever since. The Christmas tree in the fireplace is cut from a tiny segment of an old damaged quilt.

However, if there is one thing more I would add to this quilt that I didn't think of until too late, it would be a stack of books under the Christmas tree. Gary and I and all three of my children are prolific readers with large personal libraries. My fantasy is that Santa is weary and is at the LAST house and, obviously, quite anxious to get to his home to his Mrs.; hence the "thought bubble."

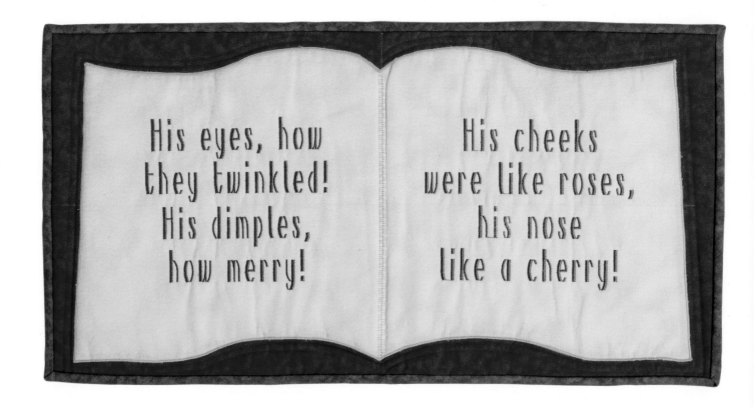

Shannon Shirley, Woodbridge, Virginia

Wool, and cotton, hand appliquéd, hand embroidered, tulle overlay, crystal embellishments, intense watercolor pencil, machine quilted

When I began this project, it was my intention to just use wool felt, but I wasn't happy with the lack of texture in the beard, so I added wool roving. I then realized how much it would shed, and, since this quilt was going to travel, I needed to cover it with tulle to minimize that problem. The entire piece is hand embroidered since I find blanket stitch very relaxing. I used Derwent Inktense Watercolor Pencils to add the rosy color to his cheeks and nose. The final detail was to add two crystals for the twinkle in his eyes.

The ball at the end of Santa's cap is a miniature Winding Ways quilt. I have a Winding Ways quilt above my mantel and wanted to incorporate it in this stanza quilt since it is also in my stanza 25 quilt. Merry Christmas.

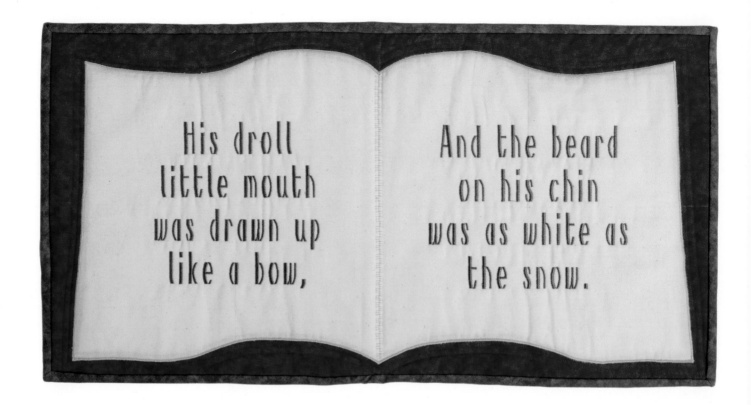

Mary Walter, Southborough, Massachusetts

Cotton, hand dyed fabric, machine pieced, hand embroidered, big-stitch quilting, embellished couched beard

When I envisioned an old-fashioned Santa Claus, I thought of a Scandinavian Santa making his way through the piney starlit woods to visit sleeping children. His hooded red wool cloak and wild white beard are a welcome sight to anyone who chanced to see him in the wee hours delivering gifts.

I made a background of pieced pine trees with a border of holly and vines to appliqué on my Santa. I used embroidery to create the details on Santa's face. His textured beard was a combination of an appliquéd white base fabric with torn, knotted, and couched strips of fabric sewn in swirls. The materials I used were commercial cotton and my own hand dyed cotton fabric.

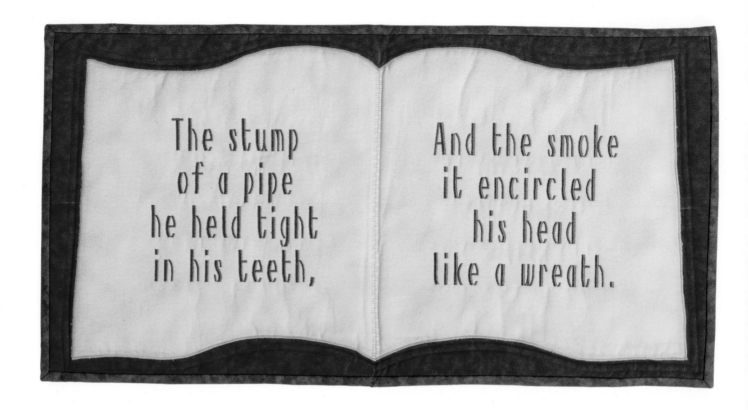

The stump of a pipe he held tight in his teeth,

And the smoke it encircled his head like a wreath.

Bunnie Jordan, Vienna, Virginia

Cotton, angel hair fibers, roving, netting, organza, paint sticks, machine pieced, machine appliquéd, and machine quilted

Clement Moore's world-famous poem includes this stanza, and numerous images and prints through time provided inspiration. Though some modern print versions may have deleted these few lines, St. Nick's pipe smoking seems right in keeping with other Victorian customs no longer practiced. I deliberately made the pipe a little dramatic to help place it in the past. The smoke incorporates several materials, several techniques, and several experiments. Santa's bag of toys is made from a recycled 1980s miniature quilt and cutouts from several themed fabrics. Additional piecing was used on the bag strap and jacket front.

*The Night Before Christmas*, illustrations by Jessie Wilcox Smith (Boston and New York: Houghton Mifflin, 1912)

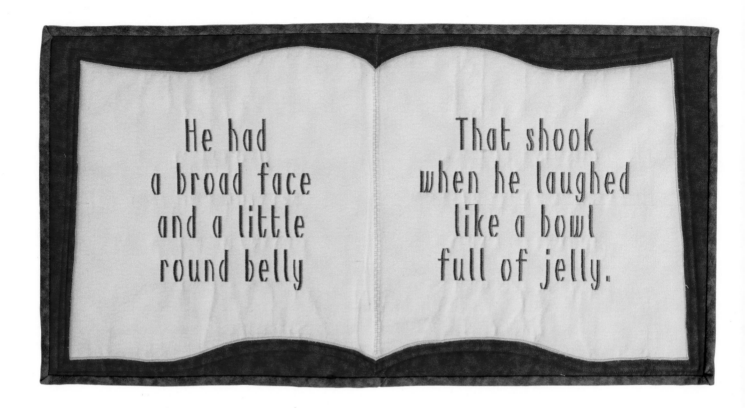

He had
a broad face
and a little
round belly

That shook
when he laughed
like a bowl
full of jelly.

Barb Vedder, Madison, Connecticut

Cotton, machine pieced and machine appliquéd, machine quilted

When I started this project, I reflected on the memories and decorations of my childhood. My family had a collection of Santa's elves that were round, with pointed flocked paper hats and black wooden feet. They all wore this expression of mirth.

The *Peanuts* Christmas special (*A Charlie Brown Christmas*) inspired my tree. As a young girl, I marveled at the aluminum tree park full of tall, brightly colored trees.

I included bubblegum pink because my Christmases always included a lot of new pink Barbie gifts.

*The Night Before Christmas*, drawings by Margaret Evans Price (Rochester, NY: Stecher Litho., 1917)

He was chubby and plump, a right jolly old elf,

And I laughed when I saw him, in spite of myself.

Bonnie Dwyer, Manchester, Maine

Cotton and metallic-coated fabric, machine pieced and machine appliquéd, embellished with fur and googly eyes, machine quilted

I wanted to create a very simple, "modern" Santa, and to make it a bit humorous. When I found a chubby, elf-like Santa image created from just a circle, I knew immediately it would achieve my goal. The googly eyes added a little humor. Then, I found in my fabric scraps a very small piece of "cheater," or preprinted patchwork, and used it for Santa's sack, thus fulfilling the requirement to include some patchwork. I hope this one makes you smile.

Sheet music featuring a quilt, ca. 1923

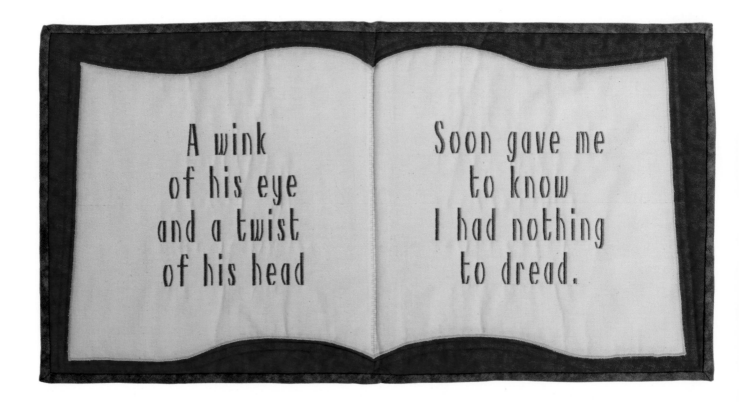

Mary Kerr, Woodbridge, Virginia

Cotton, machine pieced and machine appliquéd, embellished with sequins, buttons, rickrack, tatting, metallic thread, and a zipper

I was inspired to create this collage quilt when I found this vintage Santa stocking from circa 1950. I loved the quirkiness of the sequins and the felted texture. I paired fragments of a vintage red-and-white top with a cutter quilt base, both circa 1900. Vintage rickrack and buttons were added with additional sparkles. Not exactly a wink, but a nod to the jolly elf who just makes me smile!

*The Night Before Christmas*, drawings by Margaret Evans Price (Rochester, NY: Stecher Litho., 1917)

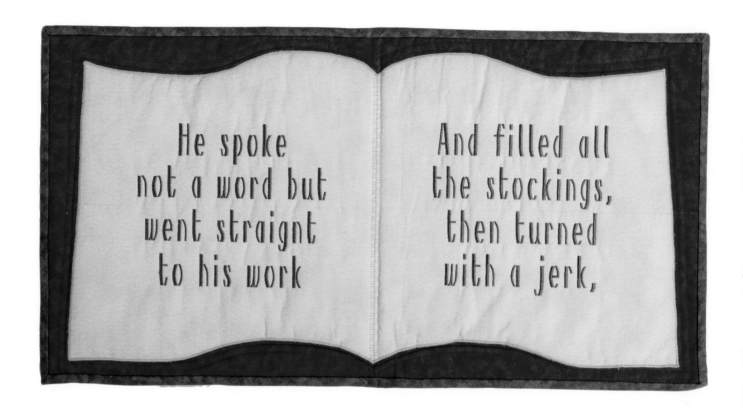

He spoke
not a word but
went straignt
to his work

And filled all
the stockings,
then turned
with a jerk,

Shannon Shirley, Woodbridge, Virginia

Cotton; hand and machine appliquéd; hand embroidered; embellished with buttons, vintage linens, ribbon, tatting, beading, and ruching; machine quilted

I love to incorporate vintage textiles into the quilts I make, and this one is no different. Vintage orphan blocks, dresser scarves, chenille bedspread, trim, tatting, and part of a cutter quilt were used in the piece. Miniature quilt designs can be found in the Winding Ways background and Santa's sack of presents. A nativity scene represents the true meaning of Christmas.

*The Night Before Christmas,* drawings by Margaret Evans Price
(Rochester, NY: Stecher Litho., 1917)

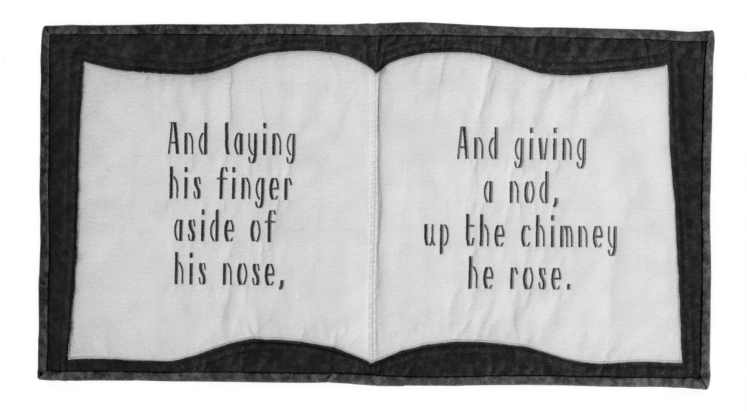

Brenda Joy Grampas, Brooksville, Florida

Cotton; hand appliquéd; machine pieced; hand embroidered; embellished with beading, vintage doilies, and metallic cord; hand quilted

The challenge was to include "patchwork" in the piece, and I began there. Being a traditional quilter, I knew immediately I wanted "Irish Chain" wallpaper with a fireplace and floor area at the bottom. I planned a Christmas tree to one side with Santa front and center. I planned the wall, fireplace, and floor background, and it was on my design wall for over a year as I searched and auditioned appropriate fabrics and embellishments for the details.

This piece includes needle-turn appliqué, using fussy cuts from specialty fabrics. Santa's wool suit is raw-edge appliqué with hand inked details. Santa's face is hand drawn. His hair, beard, and eyebrows are Brazilian embroidery: "bullion" stitches. The holly branches are hand embroidery with hand beaded berries. I included vintage doilies to serve as rug and tree skirt.

The tree was a challenge. Working with miniature log cabin blocks provides an additional patchwork element. Christmas is a special time, and I was able to express my traditional impressions of this classic poem. The center of each log cabin block is of a bright color to represent ornaments.

*The Night Before Christmas*, "Profusely Illustrated" (Chicago and New York: M. A. Donahue, 1918)

He sprang
to his sleigh,
to his team
gave a whistle,

And away
they all flew
like the down
of a thistle.

Karen Dever, Moorestown, New Jersey; Janet Cohen, Cherry Hill, New Jersey

Cotton; machine appliquéd; embellished with bells, chains, metallic threads, ribbon, ornaments, presents, beads, and a clock; machine quilted

Once I heard that I was going to be included in this project, I knew to ask for the help of my friend Janet Cohen. This was to be a collaboration between a "traditional" quilter and a more experienced "art quilter" whom I had met after joining the Needle and Gun Quilt Club. When we knew what stanza was to be ours, we knew immediately that we would use a technique of Judith Reilly of Vermont to create the houses that our Santa would fly over! Janet drew the life-size picture of the quilt we were to create, then we began cutting the design apart for our templates. Janet painted the face of our Santa. We purchased earrings for the "whistle" that arrived from England, and charms to be toys coming out of his sack. I learned how to use Angelina fiber and adding beads for the down of the thistle. I found precut and prefused reindeer online—what a score! If you look closely, you will see that our miniature quilt is in Santa's sack—that was certainly a challenge for me! Our alliance worked, and we had lots of laughs when together to create our unique quilt for this book and celebration.

*The Night Before Christmas*, drawings by Margaret Evans Price (Rochester, NY: Stecher Litho., 1917)

Alma R. Moates, Pensacola, Florida

Cotton, machine pieced and machine appliquéd, machine quilted

I was pleased to get the opportunity to be a part of this quilt project. "The Night before Christmas" has always been a favorite part of our family Christmas. All of the patterns used in this quilt are my own. My interpretation of Santa's departure is set in present-day rural America. As the "man of the house" watches Santa fly out of sight, he stands on a second-floor balcony wrapped in a quilt. Santa did not forget the woodland creatures. He placed presents for them under an old tree in the backyard.

*The Night Before Christmas*, illustrated by Fern Bisel Peat (Akron, OH: Saalfield, 1936)

# KEEPING QUILTS IN
# CHRISTMAS

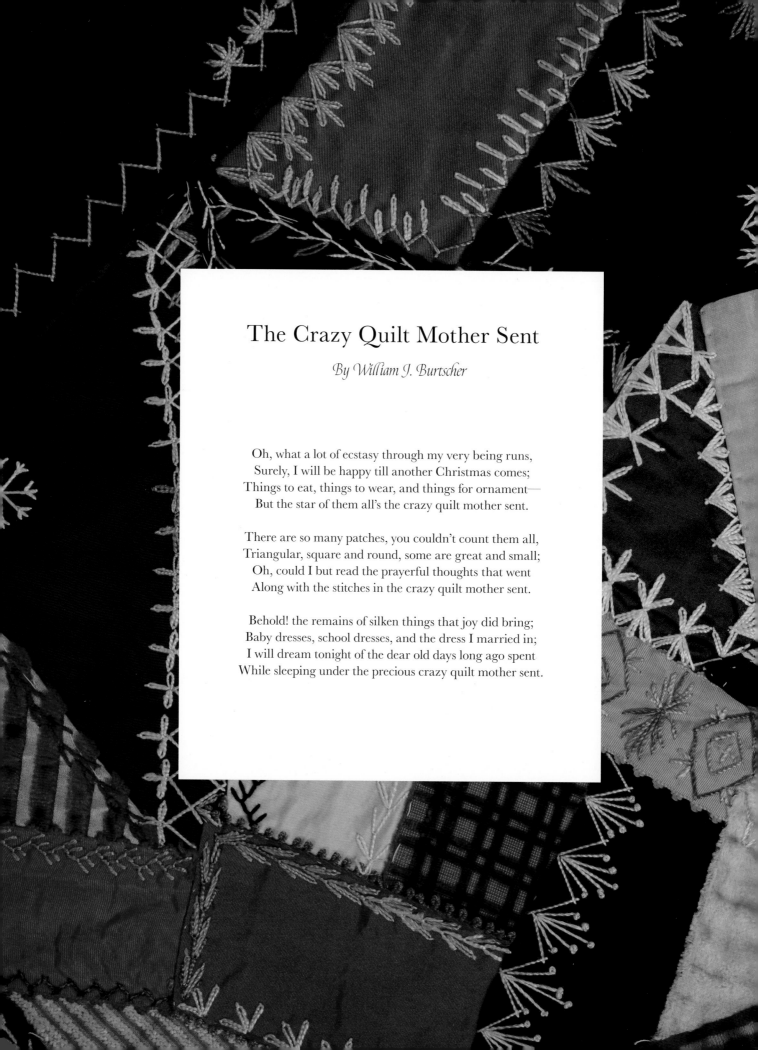

# The Crazy Quilt Mother Sent

*By William J. Burtscher*

Oh, what a lot of ecstasy through my very being runs,
Surely, I will be happy till another Christmas comes;
Things to eat, things to wear, and things for ornament—
But the star of them all's the crazy quilt mother sent.

There are so many patches, you couldn't count them all,
Triangular, square and round, some are great and small;
Oh, could I but read the prayerful thoughts that went
Along with the stitches in the crazy quilt mother sent.

Behold! the remains of silken things that joy did bring;
Baby dresses, school dresses, and the dress I married in;
I will dream tonight of the dear old days long ago spent
While sleeping under the precious crazy quilt mother sent.

Since the 1990s, when I set a goal to cover my family's bed with Christmas quilts, I never anticipated including them in a book about "'Twas the Night Before Christmas."

*Pot of Tulips quilt block, ca. 1900*

*Cottage Tulips Quilt, ca. 1935*

*Alice Brooks' quilt pattern "Anemones," ca. 1940*

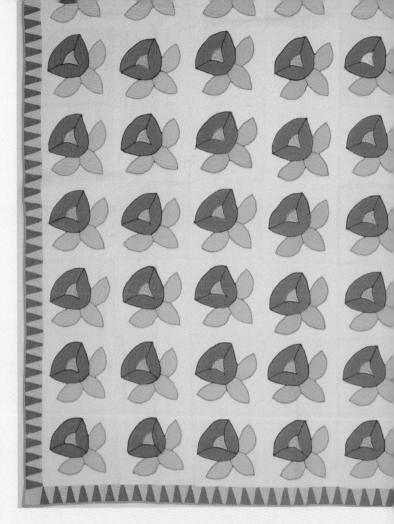

RIGHT: Late 19th Century Nine Patch quilt paired with a Turkey Red print dress from the Christmas decor of Ann Hermes, Ambler, PA

BELOW: Red and green antique quilts from the collection of Ann Hermes, Ambler, PA

Now, as we celebrate the two hundredth commemorative year of the epic holiday poem, sharing those quilts seems very appropriate. In addition to the usual holiday decor, my family's beds are now covered with red-and-green quilts.

ABOVE: Detail of a late-19th-century New England quilt featuring the famed Thomas Nast Santa

RIGHT: The festive, Christmasy home of Madge Ziegler, Newark, DE

Over the years, newly made Christmas quilts have been gifted to children and grandchildren alike. Antique and vintage red-and-green quilts also add to the trimmings around the Christmas tree. Many of my quilt friends also decorate with antique and new quilts during the Christmas season. I would like to thank Ann Hermes and Madge Zeigler for sharing the newly made and antique and vintage quilts ornamenting their Christmas merriments.

# Christmastide Quilt
## PATTERNS

Patterns redesigned by Ann Parsons Holte

# DASHER

Finished size: approx. 74" × 82" | 4" border at top and bottom of quilt | 25 10⅝" finished-size blocks
2½" finished width sashing width

## FABRIC REQUIREMENTS

5 yards red
   Blocks: 3 yards
   Quilt side-setting & quilt corner triangles: 1⅜ yards
   Top/bottom borders: ⅝ yard

4 yards white
   Blocks: 2 yards
   Sashing & cornerstones: 2 yards

**BACKING:** 82" × 91"
**BINDING:** ¾ yard

## CUTTING

### Borders, Quilt Side-Setting Triangles, and Quilt Corner Triangles

From red, cut and set aside
- 2 4½" × approx. 85" strips (A). Exact measurement will be determined after top is pieced.
- 3 23⅜" squares for quilt side-setting triangles (B)

2 12" squares for quilt corner triangles (C)

### Sashing and Cornerstones

From white, cut and set aside
- 64 11⅛" × 3" pieces for sashing (H)
- 40 3" squares for cornerstones (I)

### Blocks

#### From red, cut
- 200 2" × 3½" rectangles for flying-goose units (E)
- 100 2⅝" squares for block corner units (F)
- 50 2⅝" squares cut in half on the diagonal for block center square-in-square corners (G)
- 25 7⅞" squares cut in half TWICE on the diagonal for block side-setting triangles (D)

#### From white, cut
- 400 2" squares for flying-goose units (J)
- 100 2⅝" squares cut in half on the diagonal for block corner units (K)
- 25 2⅝" squares for block center square-in-square (L)

## MAKING THE 25 BLOCKS

### Make 200 Flying-Goose Units

You will need
- 200 red 2" × 3 ½" rectangles (E)
- 400 white 2" squares (J)

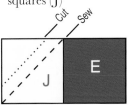

Draw a diagonal line from corner to corner on the back of each 2" square.

Place one square right sides together, with the red rectangle at one end.

Sew on the drawn line.

Trim, leaving ¼" seam allowance.

Press seam allowance open or toward rectangle.

Repeat with second square on the other end of rectangle, pressing seam allowance away from rectangle.

Unit should measure 2" × 3½".

**Make 100 Block Corner Units**
You will need
- 100 red 2⅝" squares (F)
- 100 white 2⅝" squares, cut in half on the diagonal (K)

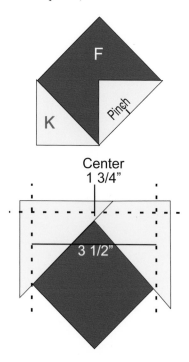

**Make 25 Center Square-in-Square Units**
You will need
- 25 white 2⅝" squares (L)
- 50 red 2⅝" squares cut in half on diagonal (G)

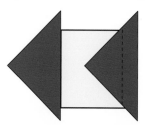

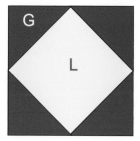

Find the center of one side of the red square; pinch to make a crease to mark the center.

Fold one white triangle to find center of long edge; pinch.

Align the centers of the sides and stitch ¼" seam allowance.

Press seam open.

Repeat with second white triangle and adjacent side of red square.

The unit is slightly oversized and will need to be trimmed.

Trim edge, leaving ¼" from point to raw edge.

Next, trim sides to measure 3½" wide, being sure to measure 1¾" from the center so that the point is midway between the two sides.

Made in the same way as the block corner units, except that the first two triangles are added to opposite sides of the square.

Next, two triangles are added to the remaining sides.

Trim the unit to 3½" square, again making sure to leave ¼" seam allowance beyond the points of the center square.

## ASSEMBLING THE 25 BLOCKS

For each of the blocks, make 4 units from
- 1 block corner unit and
- 2 flying-goose units

Cut the 7⅝" red (D) squares into quarters on the diagonal.

Assemble the block as illustrated

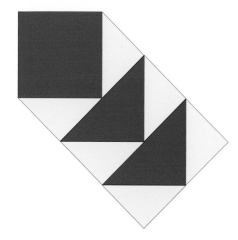

## ASSEMBLING THE QUILT

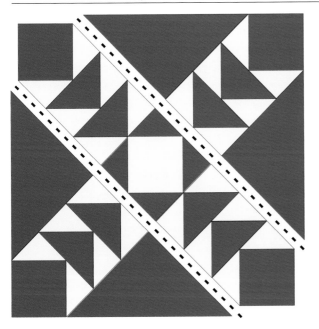

This quilt will go together in 7 diagonal rows. The blocks are separated by sashing pieces and cornerstones. Quilt side-setting triangles and quilt corners are added as indicated.

You will need
- 64 11⅛" × 3" sashing rectangles (H)
- 40 3" cornerstone squares (I)
- 3 23⅜" squares, cut twice on diagonal for quilt side-setting triangles (B)
- 2 12" squares, cut once on diagonal for quilt corners (C)

Attach the 4 quilt corners after the quilt is assembled.

Trim off cornerstones that fall on the edge of the quilt.

Measure finished quilt to find the correct measurements for the top and bottom borders.

Cut the borders to the measured length, which should be about 74½"–75".

# DANCER

Finished size: 84½" × 84½" | 169 6½" finished-size blocks

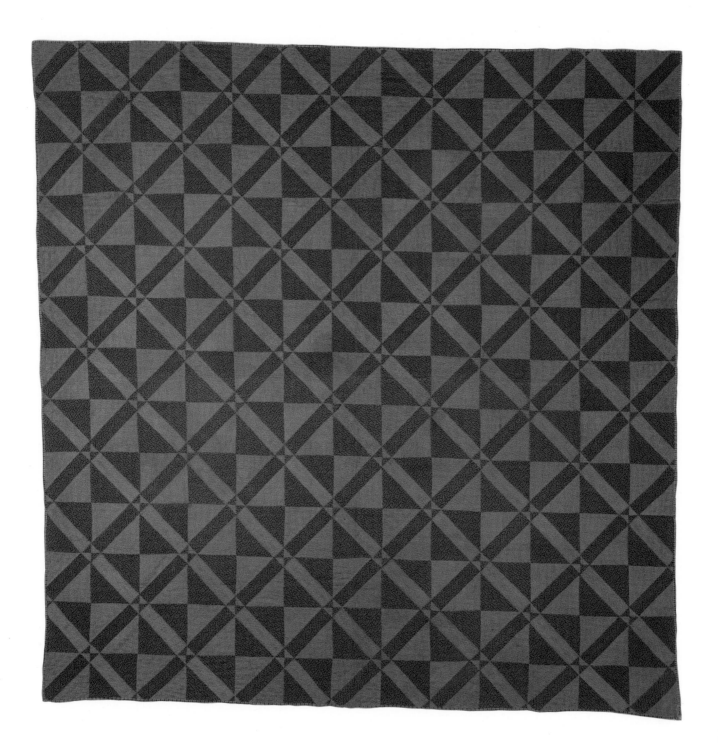

## FABRIC REQUIREMENTS

4½ yards red
4½ yards green

**BACKING**: 92" × 92"
**BINDING**: ¾ yard

## CUTTING

There is only one block for this quilt, but the colors are reversed and the blocks are oriented to create the secondary designs.

**From red, cut**
- 85 6½" squares
- 84 2" × 10" rectangles
- 170 1½" squares

**From green, cut**
- 84 6½" squares
- 85 2" × 10" rectangles
- 168 1½" squares

## MARKING

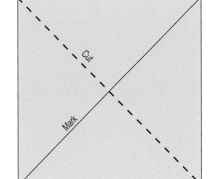

Marking the back of the squares and rectangles will help you assemble the blocks and square them up.

For both sizes of squares, use a pencil to mark one diagonal line on the wrong side.

Set aside the small squares.

Cut the large squares in half on the diagonal PERPENDICULAR to the drawn line.

On the back of the rectangles, mark a line through the centers, lengthways and crossways.

## MAKING THE BLOCKS

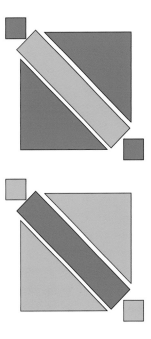

Each block will require 1 large square (cut in half on diagonal), 2 small squares, and 1 rectangle.

The large and small squares are of the same color.

The rectangle will be of the other color.

You will make 85 squares with red corners and 84 squares with green corners.

## Attach Large Triangles to Center Rectangle

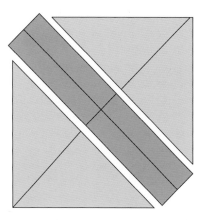

Match the crossways centerline of the rectangle to the centerline of a triangle.

Sew right sides together along the edges, with a ¼" seam.

Repeat with the other triangle on the other long edge of the rectangle.

Press seams open.

## Square Up the Blocks

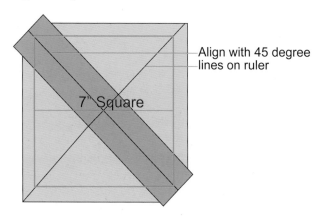

Align with 45 degree lines on ruler

7" Square

Use the diagonal drawn lines to square up the block to 7".

Use the lines you drew after cutting the squares to help you line up the block for squaring.

## Add the Corners

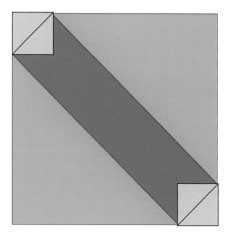

Place the small square at the end of the rectangle, at the corners of the block, so that the drawn line touches the adjacent edges of the fabric, as shown.

Sew on the drawn line.

Trim away the excess corner, leaving ¼" seam allowance.

Press seam open.

Repeat with square at the other end of the rectangle.

## ASSEMBLING THE QUILT

Attach the blocks into 13 rows, alternating both the color and the direction of the rectangle.

Note that in the original quilt, all the green rectangles are oriented on the diagonal upper left / lower right.

The red rectangles are oriented on the diagonal upper right / lower left.

Press the seams open as you attach the blocks.

Be careful matching the seams so that the secondary design of quarter-square triangles appears at the intersections of the blocks.

You might find it easier to attach the rows in pairs and then attach the pairs together until you get to the last row, which is a single row.

# PRANCER

Finished size: approx. 89" square | 2" border | 13 20" finished-size blocks

Side Setting Triangles

Corner Triangles

**Setting Triangles**

From background, cut and set aside

- 2 21⅝" squares for quilt side-setting triangles. Cut these squares in half TWICE on diagonal. Label these "side-setting triangles."
- 2 15⅛" squares for quilt corner triangles. Cut these squares in half ONCE on diagonal. Label these "corner triangles."

The original quilt top that inspired this design was made in the early 1900s and had a couple of quirks. First, some of the fabric used in this quilt was dyed with a red that turned out to be fugitive: some of the triangles that should have been red are now a buff color. Second, the red + green half-square triangle units are not all oriented the same way: some have the red half pointing toward the center of the block, which is traditional; others are oriented differently. It is your choice to make the quilt in the perfectly oriented, traditional manner, or to throw in some off-color and oddly turned HST units. Sometimes mistakes make for a lively quilt.

*Note: You will need 624 2" finished-size red + green half-square triangle units for this quilt. These instructions are for using the "Eight-at-a-Time" method, which produces no waste and exactly the right-size units. You may decide to use a different technique.

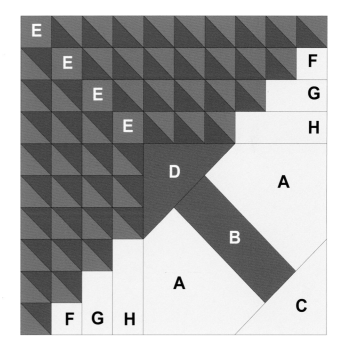

## FABRIC REQUIREMENTS

2¼ yards red for blocks
2¾ yards green for blocks
1⅜ yards brown for blocks
4¾ yards background fabric
    3¼ yards for blocks
    1½ yards for side-setting & corner triangles
¾ yard for 2" border

    **BACKING**: 97" square
    **BINDING**: ¾ yard

**Blocks**

For 12" trunk blocks, cut

- 13 12" squares of background (A)
- 13 3⅜" × 18" rectangles brown (B)
- 13 6½" squares background (C)
- 13 6½" squares brown (D)

For trees, cut
- 78 5¾" squares from red (*See note above)
- 78 5¾" squares from green (*See note above)
- 52 2½" squares from green (E)

Cut 9 2½" strips across WOF from background.

Cut strips into
- 26 2½" squares (F)
- 26 2½" × 4½" rectangles (G)
- 26 2½" × 6½" rectangles (H)

## MAKING THE 13 TREE BLOCKS

### Make Half-Square Triangle Units by Using the Eight-at-a-Time Method

On the 5¾" squares, draw an X from corner to corner on the back of the lighter fabric.

Layer together one red and one green square, right sides together.

Sew ¼" from the line on each side.

Press to set the seams.

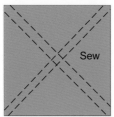

See illustration for cut #1.

Try not to disturb the fabric when you make cut #2.

Press seam allowances toward darker fabric or open.

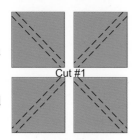

### Make Trunk Units

Make a light mark on the back of a 12½" background (A) square at the center.

Cut square in half on the diagonal.

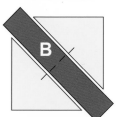

Find the center of the 3⅜" × 18" brown (B) strip.

Attach the strip to the split square, matching the center on each half.

Press seam allowance toward brown fabric.

Retrim the square to 12½".

Draw a diagonal line from corner to corner on the back of the 6½" brown (D) and background (C) squares.

Place the squares, right sides together, at opposite ends of the trunk, as shown.

Sew ON the drawn line.

Cut off corners, leaving ¼" seam allowance, & press seam allowance open.

## ASSEMBLING BLOCK UNITS

Pay attention to the orientation of the half-square triangles as you put this block together.

Notice that the red half always "points toward" the diagonal center of the block.

You will assemble 13 of each of the block units and attach them to form the 20" finished-size block.

## ASSEMBLING THE QUILT

Attach the tree blocks to the side-setting triangles and corner triangles, as shown in the diagram.

Attach the diagonal rows as shown in the diagram below.

Measure the finished top through the center to get an accurate measurement for the outer border.

Cut 4 2½" red strips to this measurement.

Attach 2 strips to the left and right sides.

Cut 4 2½" green corner squares and add to the ends of the two remaining strips.

Attach the top and bottom borders.

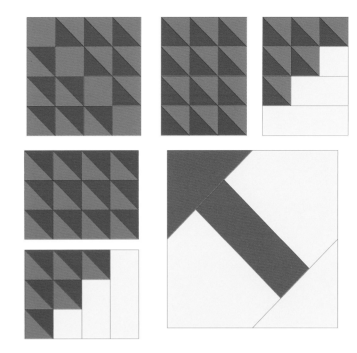

# VIXEN

Finished size: 72" × 90" | 3 3" borders | 12 18" finished-size blocks

Note: You will need 96 3" finished-size red + green and 48 3" finished-size red + white half-square triangle units for this quilt. These instructions are for using the "Eight-at-a-Time" method, which produces no waste and exactly the right-size units. You may decide to use a different technique.

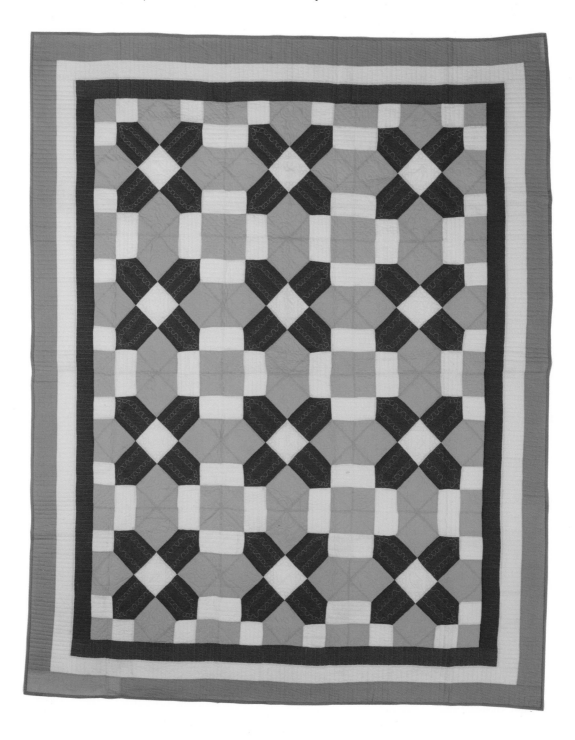

## FABRIC REQUIREMENTS

1⅝ yards red for blocks
2⅞ yards green for blocks
1⅞ yards white for blocks
⅞ yard for 3" red border
¾ yard for 3" green border
⅞ yard for 3" white border

**BACKING:** 80" × 98"
**BINDING:** ¾ yard

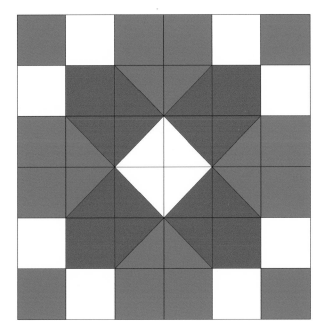

## CUTTING

Note: WOF means "width of fabric"—generally 40"+

### Blocks

**From green, cut**
- 20 3½" strips across WOF
    Cut these strips into 216 3½" squares.
- 4 7¾" strips across WOF
    Cut these strips into 18 7¾" squares.

**From red, cut**
- 7 3½" strips across WOF
    Cut these strips into 72 3½" squares.
- 2 7¾" strips across WOF
    Cut these strips into 18 7¾" squares.

**From white, cut**
- 13 3½" strips across WOF
    Cut these strips into 144 3½" squares.
- 2 7¾" strips across WOF
    Cut these strips into 9 7¾" squares.

### Borders
#### From green
- Cut and piece, end to end, 8 3½" × WOF strips.
    Cut these strips into
    —2 3½" × 84½" borders (left/right)
    —2 3½" × 72½" borders (top/bottom)

#### From red
- Cut and piece, end to end, 7 3½" × WOF strips.
    Cut these strips into
    —2 3½" × 72½" borders (left/right)
    —2 3½" × 60½" borders (top/bottom)

#### From white
- Cut 8 3½" × WOF strips.
    Cut these strips into
    —2 3½" × 78½" borders (left/right)
    —2 3½" × 72½" borders (top/bottom)

## MAKING THE BLOCKS

### Make Half-Square Triangle Units by Using Eight-at-a-Time Method

Use 18 red and 18 green 7¾" squares to make 144 red + green HSTs

Use 9 red and 9 white 7¾" Squares to make 72 red + white HSTs

Draw an X from corner to corner on the back of the lighter fabric.

Layer together one red and one green square.

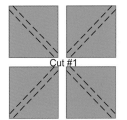

Sew ¼" from the line on each side.

Press to set the seams.

See illustration for cut #1.

Try not to disturb the fabric when you make cut #2.

Press seam allowances toward darker fabric or open.

**Assemble the Blocks**

Use the 3½" red, green, and white squares to make 96 9-patch units as illustrated.

Each block uses 4 of these 9-patch units, with each of the units turned ¼ turn.

## ASSEMBLING THE QUILT

Attach the 12 blocks in 4 rows of 3 blocks each, as shown.
Attach the borders, starting with the red left/right borders.
In the same way, attach the white and green borders.

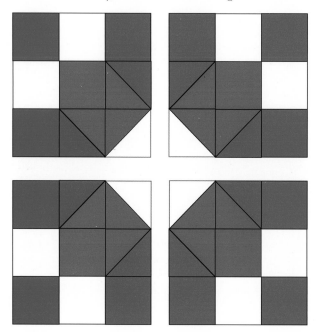

# COMET

Finished size: 56" × 70" | 20 14" blocks

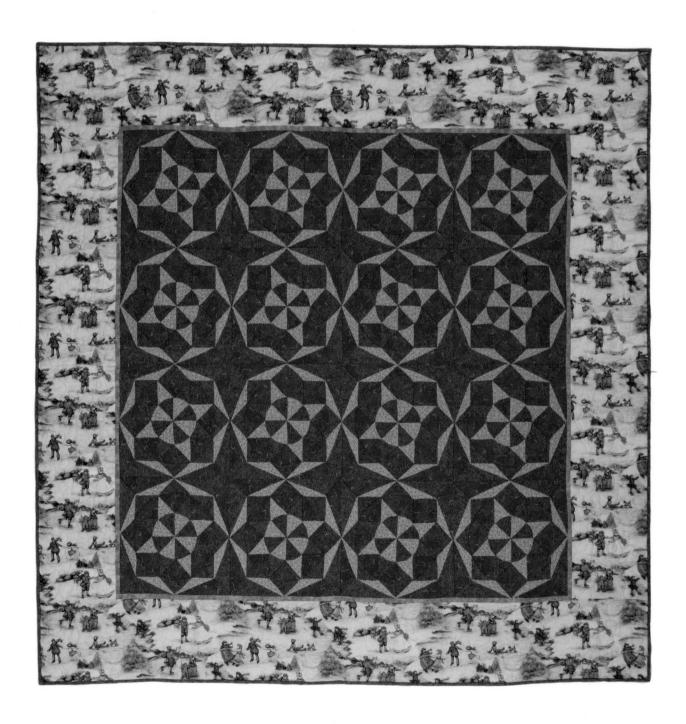

## FABRIC REQUIREMENTS

3¾ yards green
2 yards red
2½ yards white

**BINDING:** ¾ yard
**BACKING:** 64" × 78"

Extra fabric will be needed for borders and for fussy-cutting or matching stripes.

## CUTTING

Refer to the "Making Templates" section for instructions. Acrylic templates can be ordered separately from AnnHolteQuilting.com.

For each single block, you will need
- 8 green A
- 8 red B
- 4 white C
- 4 green C
- 4 white D
- 4 green D
- 8 white E
- 4 green F
- 4 red F reversed

For the 20-block quilt, a good idea is to cut the fabric into WOF (width of fabric) strips and then cut the shapes from those strips.

| Template | Fabric | WOF Strips | Pieces |
|---|---|---|---|
| A | green | 10 3½" | 160 |
| B | red | 10 3½" | 160 |
| C | green | 10 2¾" | 80 |
| C | white | 10 2¾" | 80 |
| D | green | 10 2¾" | 80 |
| D | white | 10 2¾" | 80 |
| E | white | 16 1¾" | 160 |
| F | green | 10 2¾" | 80 |
| F rev.* | red | 10 2¾" | 80 |

*Note: Because F is the only piece that is reversed (turn template facedown), you can cut multiple shapes from stacked layers of fabric, but not folded layers. In this color plan, all the red F pieces are reversed. The green F pieces are not reversed.

## MAKING THE BLOCKS

### By Hand

If you traced your homemade templates onto the back of the fabric, you will sew on the drawn lines when piecing by hand. When you hand piece, you can attach the pieces in almost any order because each seam is independent.

Sewing one block at a time makes this a very portable project.

### By Machine

If you cut the pieces by using the acrylic template set, which includes seam allowance, be sure to sew an accurate ¼" seam on your machine.

When you machine piece this block, it is possible to chain-piece pairs of units and then put them together.

Press seam allowances open to reduce bulk at the intersections.

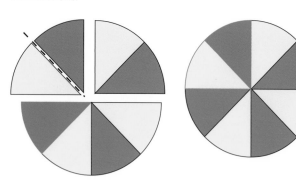

Make the center circle from the eight D pieces, alternating the colors.

Construct the first ring section from the B and C pieces.

Set the center circle into the first ring, being careful to align the colors.

Construct the second ring section from the A and E pieces.

Set the center + first ring into the second ring.

Finally, add the F and F reversed pieces to make the corners and square the block.

## ASSEMBLING THE QUILT

Attach the blocks in 5 rows of 4 blocks each.

Press the seam allowances open when you attach blocks and rows.

Be particularly careful about matching intersections.

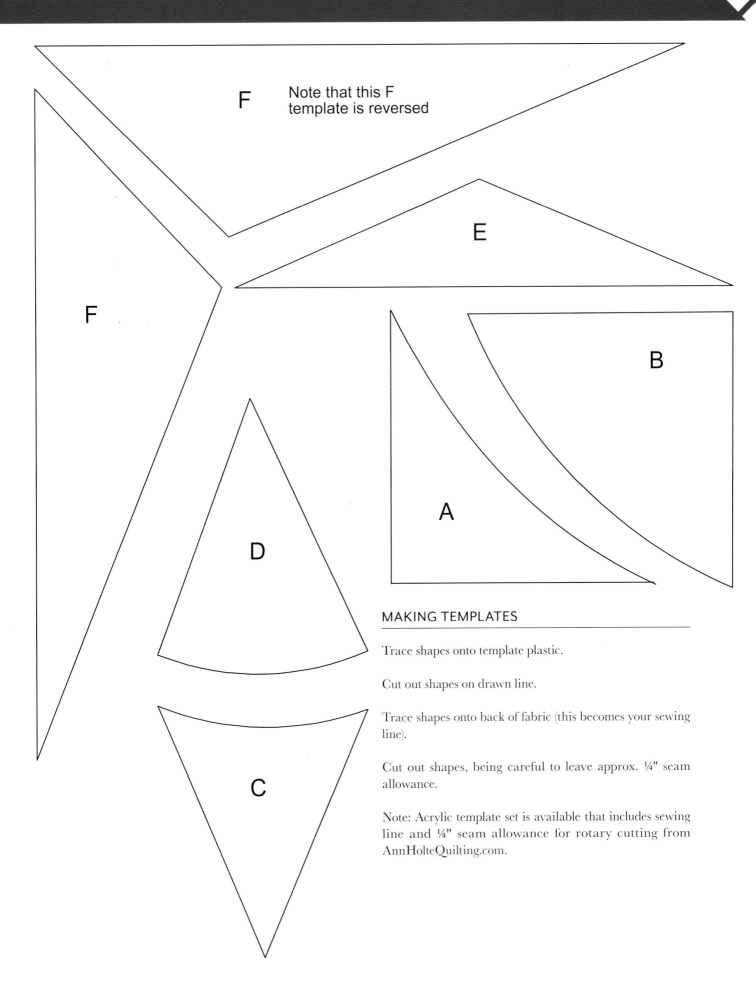

F

Note that this F
template is reversed

E

F

B

A

D

MAKING TEMPLATES

Trace shapes onto template plastic.

Cut out shapes on drawn line.

Trace shapes onto back of fabric (this becomes your sewing line).

Cut out shapes, being careful to leave approx. ¼" seam allowance.

Note: Acrylic template set is available that includes sewing line and ¼" seam allowance for rotary cutting from AnnHolteQuilting.com.

C

# CUPID

Finished size: 77" × 91" | 1 3" sawtooth border | 30 10" finished-size blocks set on point | 20 10" finished-size alternate plain blocks

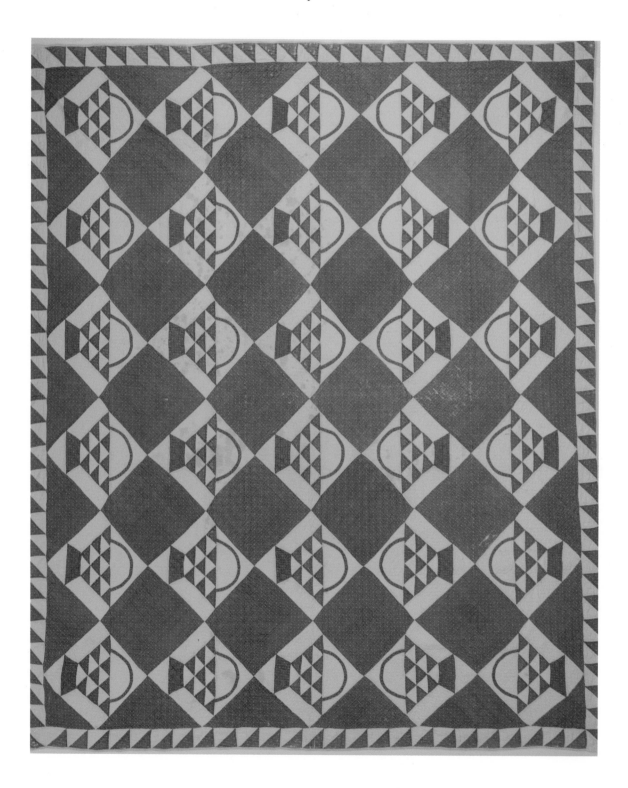

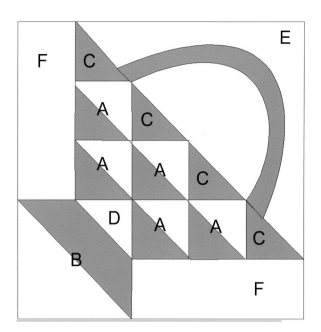

*Note about half-square triangle (HST) units:

For this quilt, you will need
- 108 3" finished-size white + green for sawtooth border
- 150 2" finished-size white + green for blocks
- 30 4" finished-size white + green for blocks

These instructions are for using the Eight-at-a-Time method for making HSTs, which produces no waste and exactly the right-size units. You may decide to use a different technique.

## FABRIC REQUIREMENTS

1⅞ yards green for blocks
2¾ yards white for blocks
1⅝ yards white for setting squares
1¾ yards white for setting triangles & corners
⅝ yard green for sawtooth border
⅝ yard white for sawtooth border

**BACKING:** 85" × 99"
**BINDING:** ¾ yard

## CUTTING

As you cut, be sure to label the pieces (A, B, C . . .) so that assembling the blocks will be easier.

**From white, cut and set aside**
- 20 10½" squares for plain blocks (J)
- 9 15½" squares, cut in half on diagonal TWICE for side-setting triangles (H)
- 2 8" squares, cut in half on diagonal ONCE for quilt corners (I)

**From green**
For basket blocks, cut
- 19 5¾" squares for 2" finished-size HSTs (A)
- 4 9¾" squares for 4" finished-size HSTs (B)
- 60 2⅞" squares, cut in half on diagonal (C)
- 30 basket handles from approx. ⅝ yard

For sawtooth border, cut
- 14 7¾" squares for 3" finished-size HSTs (G)

**From white**
For basket blocks, cut
- 19 5¾" squares for 2" finished-size HSTs (A)
- 4 9¾" squares for 4" finished-size HSTs (B)
- 30 2½" squares for corner of basket base unit (D)
- 15 8⅞" squares, cut in half on diagonal (E)
- 60 2½" × 6½" rectangles (F)

For sawtooth border, cut
- 14 7¾" squares for 3" finished-size HSTs (G)

## MAKING THE 30 BASKET BLOCKS

Use these instructions to make all Eight-at-a-Time method 2", 3", and 4" finished-size HSTs for this quilt.

Draw an X from corner to corner on the back of the lighter fabric.

Layer together one white and one green square.

Sew ¼" from the line on each side.

Press to set the seams.

See illustration for cut #1.

Try not to disturb the fabric when you make cut #2.

Press seam allowances toward darker fabric or open.

### Corner Unit

Make 30 4" finished-size green + white HSTs from the 9¾" squares (B).

Draw a diagonal line on the back of each of the 30 2½" background squares (D).

Place the 2½" square (D) on the green corner of the large HST (B).

Sew on the diagonal line and trim off the excess.

### Basket Handles

Depending on how you will apply the basket handles, trace these handle templates onto freezer paper or fusible web and follow instructions for your desired method. Notice that one template has the seam allowance and the other is actual size. Appliqué the handle to the corner triangles (E).

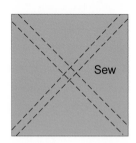
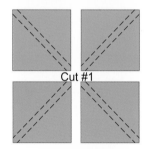

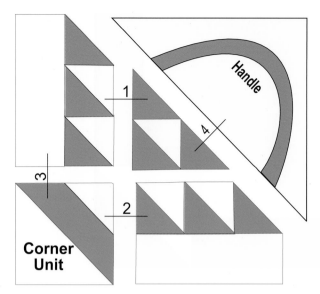

### Basket

Make 150 2" finished-size green + white HSTs from the 5¾" squares (A).

Use the 2½" × 6½" rectangles (F) along with the green (C) triangles that were cut from the 2⅞" squares to assemble the three units as illustrated.

### Sawtooth Border

Make 108 3" finished-size HST units from 7¾" squares (G).

Attach these 3" finished-size green + white HSTs, with the green corner oriented to the upper left, into (4) strips:
2 strips with 25 HST units
2 strips with 29 HST units

## ASSEMBLING THE QUILT

**Attach the blocks with quilt corners, plain blocks, and side-setting triangles in rows as illustrated.**

Notice that in the finished quilt, the blocks are arranged into 5 columns: 3 with handles oriented one way, and 2 with the handles oriented the other way.

The red handles in the illustration are to call your attention to this unusual orientation.

Attach the rows as shown.

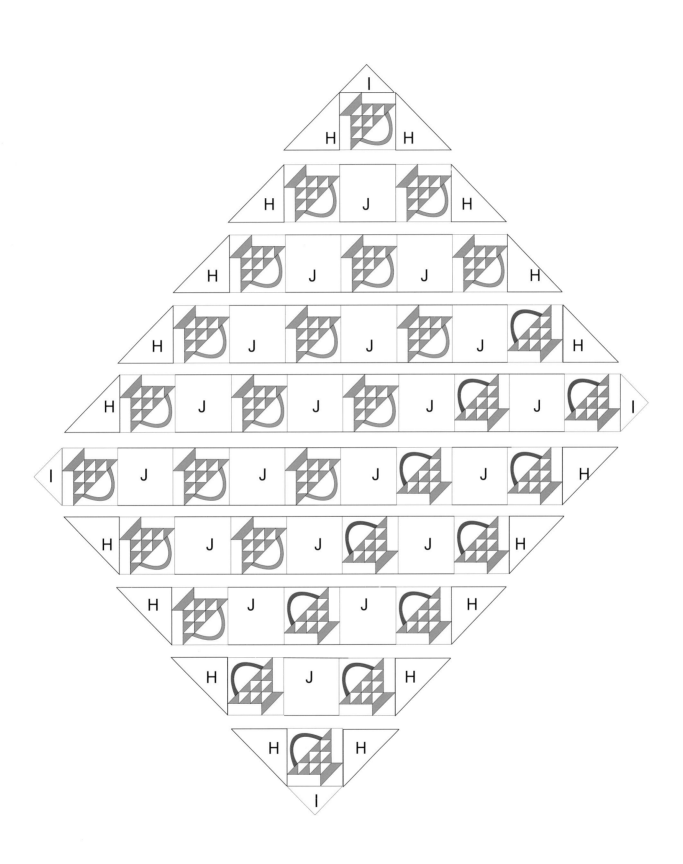

**Attach the Borders**

Apply the borders to the quilt as follows:

Attach the first 25-HST-unit border strip to the top of the quilt, leaving the first HST hanging off the left side.

Attach a 29-HST-unit border strip to the right side, starting and finishing normally.

Continue with the 25-HST-unit bottom and 29-HST-unit left borders.

Finally, complete the upper left corner of the border that was left hanging.

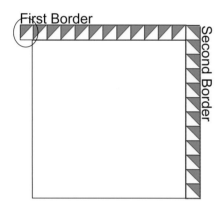

First Border

Second Border

Actual Size Handle

Handle with 1/4" seam allowance

# DONNER

Finished size: 60½" × 80"

2" finished-size inner border
4" finished-size outer border
8" finished-size hexagons measured point to point (or, 4" finished on each side)

Pattern note: The directions for the next pattern, Blitzen, are the same as this one. Only the fabric choices are different.

## NOTES ON HEXAGONS

Consider buying acrylic templates for cutting full and half hexagons (a.k.a. "hexies"). Note that there are two different kinds of half hexagons:

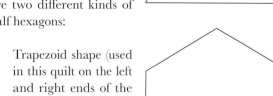

- Trapezoid shape (used in this quilt on the left and right ends of the rows)
- House shape (used to square off and finish the top and bottom of the quilt)

The full-size hexagon should measure 8" point to point for

the finished size. Each side should measure 4" finished size. Of course, a template should include the ¼" seam allowance on all sides.

Drawings are included with this pattern for you to use as a guide for making your own templates. Warning: If you use these homemade templates for making your hexagons, pin them to the fabric with flat pins and cover the template with your rotary-cutting ruler to cut alongside the template. Do not use paper or cardboard templates directly with your rotary cutter.

## FABRIC REQUIREMENTS

4¾ yards white background
2¾ yards red snowflake

½ yard red inner border
1 yard white outer border

**BACKING:** 68½" × 88"
**BINDING**: ¾ yard

## CUTTING

**From white, cut**
- 8 4½" × width of fabric (WOF = about 40") strips; set aside for outer border
- 45 whole hexies
- 7 trapezoid half hexies
- 14 house half hexies

**From red, cut**
- 8 2½" × WOF strips; set aside for inner border
- 27 whole hexies
- 3 trapezoid half hexies
- 2 house half hexies

## PIECING THE HEXAGONS

Piece the hexies together in 13 rows.

The secret to piecing hexagons is to leave ¼" unsewn, backstitching to secure the sewing line, at the beginning and end of each straight seam.

Each seam is sewn separately so that you can reposition for the next segment.

Refer to the illustration for the positioning of the red and white whole and trapezoid half hexies.

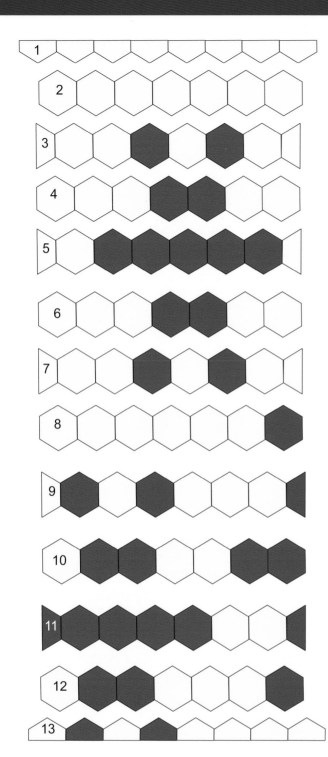

## ADDING THE BORDERS

### Attach the 2½" red strips end to end

From this long strip, cut
- 2 2½" × 72½" for left/right inner border
- 2 2½" × 53" for top/bottom inner border

Add these borders to the quilt center.

### Attach the 4½" white strips end to end

From this long strip, cut
- 2 4½" × 76½" for left/right outer border
- 2 4½" × 61" for the top/bottom outer border

Add these borders to complete the quilt top.

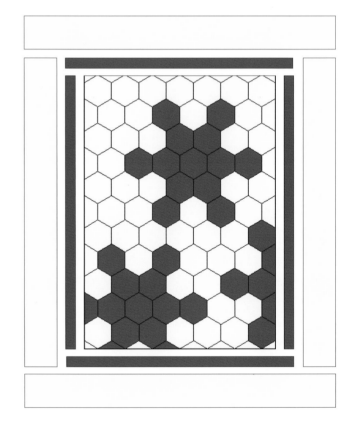

## TEMPLATES

Attach the first row to the second row, again stopping ¼" at the beginning and end of each seam.

Make two rows of house half hexies for the top and bottom of the quilt.

Notice that the first and last house half hexies on the row will hang off and will be cut down after the quilt is pieced.

Square off the four corners to remove the excess fabric.

Make three copies of this template.

Cut on the outer dashed line for a whole hexie (yellow dot marks the center).

Cut on the red dashed line for the trapezoid half hexie (used in this quilt to end the horizontal rows).

Cut on the green dashed line for the house half hexie (used in this quilt to square off the top and bottom).

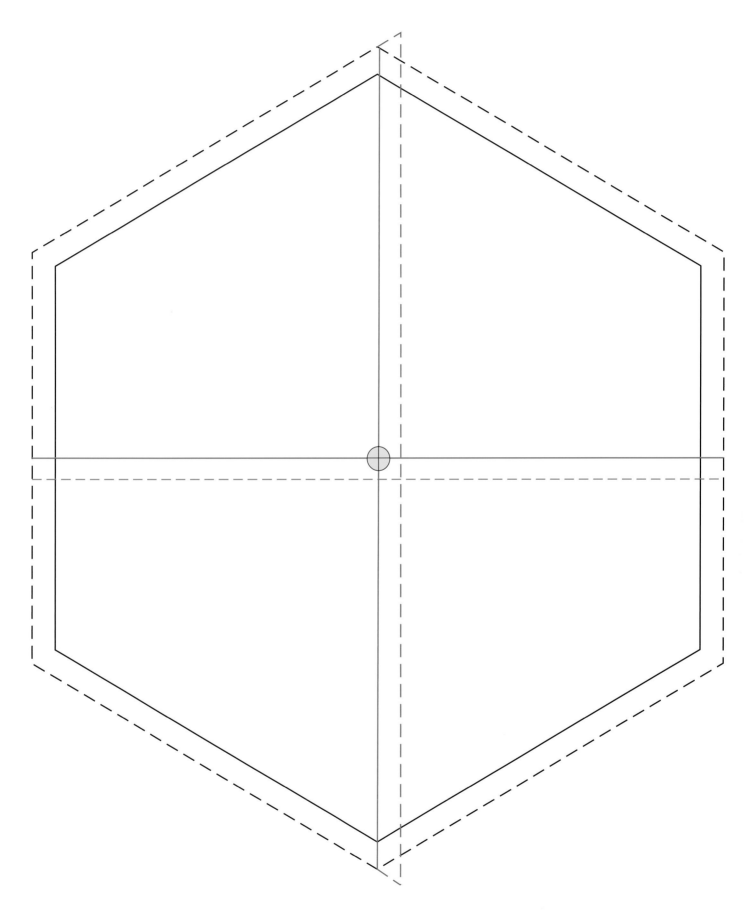

# BLITZEN

Finished size: 60½" × 80"

these homemade templates for making your hexagons, pin them to the fabric with flat pins and cover the template with your rotary-cutting ruler to cut alongside the template. Do not use paper or cardboard templates directly with your rotary cutter.

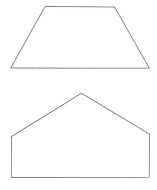

## FABRIC REQUIREMENTS

3¾ yards white background
2⅛ yards green tree
⅝ yard brown trunk
⅞ yard red ornaments
10" yellow square for star

½ yard red inner border
1 yard white outer border

**BACKING**: 68½" × 88"
**BINDING**: ¾ yard

## CUTTING

### From white, cut
* 8 4½" × width of fabric (WOF = about 40") strips; set aside for outer border
* 26 whole hexies
* 8 trapezoid half hexies
* 16 house half hexies

### From green, cut
* 30 whole hexies
* 2 trapezoid half hexies
* 2 house half hexies

### From brown, cut
* 5 whole hexies

### From red, cut
* 8 2½" × WOF strips; set aside for inner border
* 10 whole hexies

### From yellow, cut
* whole hexie

2" finished-size inner border
4" finished-size outer border
8" finished-size hexagons measured point to point (or, 4" finished on each side)

Pattern note: The directions for the previous pattern, Donner, are the same as this one. Only the fabric choices are different.

## NOTES ON HEXAGONS

Considering buying acrylic templates for cutting full and half hexagons. Note that there are two kinds of half hexagons:

* Trapezoid shape (used in this quilt on the left and right ends of the rows)
* House shape (used to square off and finish the top and bottom of the quilt)

The full-size hexagon should measure 8" point to point for the finished size. Each side should measure 4" finished size. Of course, a template should include the ¼" seam allowance on all sides.

Drawings are included with this pattern for you to use as a guide for making your own templates. Warning: If you use

## PIECING THE HEXAGONS

Piece the hexies together in 13 rows.

The secret to piecing hexagons is to leave ¼" unsewn, back-stitching to secure the sewing line, at the beginning and end of each straight seam.

Each seam is sewn separately so that you can reposition for the next segment.

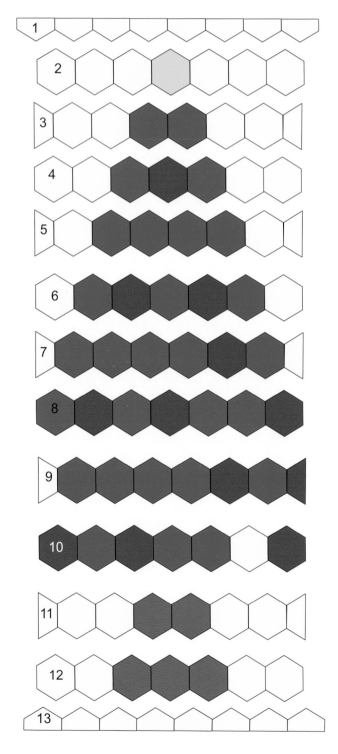

Refer to the illustration for the positioning of the red and white whole and trapezoid half hexies.

Attach the first row to the second row, again stopping ¼" at the beginning and end of each seam.

Make two rows of house half hexies for the top and bottom of the quilt.

Notice that the first and last house half hexies on the row will hang off and will be cut down after the quilt is pieced.

Square off the four corners to remove the excess fabric.

## ADDING THE BORDERS

### Attach the 2½" red strips end to end.

From this long strip, cut
- 2 2½" × 72½" for left/right inner border
- 2 2½" × 53" for top/bottom inner border

Add these borders to the quilt center.

### Attach the 4½" white strips end to end.

From this long strip, cut
- 2 4½" × 76½" for left/right outer border
- 2 4½" × 61" for the top/bottom outer border

Add these borders to complete the quilt top.

## TEMPLATES

### SEE PAGE 115 FOR TEMPLATE

Make three copies of this template.

Cut on the outer dashed line for a whole hexie (yellow dot marks the center).

Cut on the red dashed line for the trapezoid half hexie (used in this quilt to end the horizontal rows).

Cut on the green dashed line for the house half hexie (used in this quilt to square off the top and bottom).

# RUDOLPH

Finished size: 84" square

Three borders with mitered corners:
- 2½" wide red
- 1½" wide white
- 2" wide green

64 9" finished-size blocks (some will be cut into quarters or halves for the edge of the quilt)

## FABRIC REQUIREMENTS

5¼ yards white for background & border (allows enough for unpieced, mitered borders)
2¾ yards red for circles & border
2¾ yards green for circles & border

**BACKING**: 92" square
**BINDING**: ¾ yard

## CUTTING

### For Borders
4 2" × 86" white strips
4 3" × 86" red strips
4 2½" × 86" green strips

### For Blocks
Cut 64 10" white squares.

Press squares into quarters.

Use the template or a circle cutter to cut a 7" hole in each square.

Set aside the circles (holes) for another project.

### For circles, cut
- 32 8" red squares
- 32 8" green squares

Use the template or a circle cutter to cut an 8" circle from each square.

Press circles into quarters.

Discard outer square leftovers.

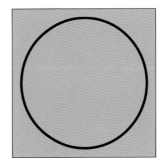 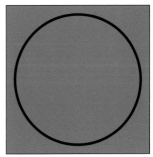

## ASSEMBLING THE BLOCKS

**Set red and green circles into the white background holes.**

With the holes and the circles creased at north, east, south, and west, place a circle and background square right side up.

Position the background right side up on top of the circle, generally aligning the pressed marks at the outer edge.

Starting at the north position, flip the top (background) over so that the right sides are together, aligning the marks, and pin.

Continue pinning at the other three creased points.

Sew ¼" seam as you feed the background and circle together.

A stiletto helps guild the fabric and hold the edges together.

Press the seam allowance inward.

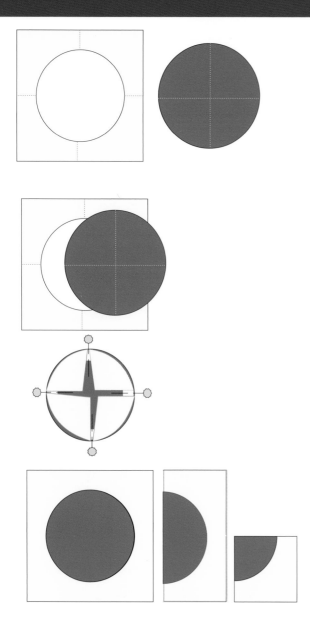

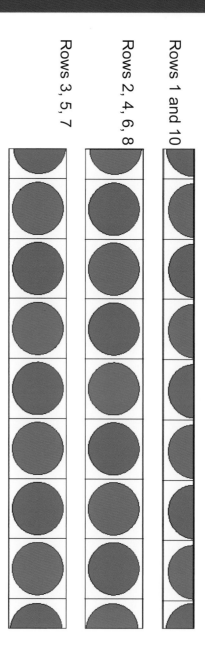

Rows 3, 5, 7

Rows 2, 4, 6, 8

Rows 1 and 10

## Trim the Blocks

Trim each of the circle blocks to 9½" square, measuring from the center of the circle.

After you have pieced and trimmed all 32 red and green (each) blocks with circle centers, you will cut down some of these to make the half and quarter circles for the edge of the quilt center.

Set aside 25 red circle blocks for body of quilt.

Set aside 24 green circle blocks for body of quilt.

Cut 1 red circle block into quarters for the four corners of the layout.

Cut 8 green circle blocks in half.

Cut 6 red circle blocks in half.

## ASSEMBLING THE QUILT

Refer to the illustration to assemble the rows.

Carefully note the placement of the red and green whole, half, and quarter blocks.

Number the rows 1 through 10 as you attach the blocks of each row.

## ADDING THE MITERED BORDER

Sew border strips together into 4 sets of three strips: red, white, and green.

Press seam allowances open.

Find center of the strip and center of quilt side.

Attach a strip set to each side of the finished top, leaving the last ¼" unsewn at each end.

Fold quilt on diagonal.

Working on one corner at a time, align and pin the seam lines where quilt body is attached to the border.

Align and pin the strips of the border so that they will meet.

Mark a 45-degree line from the point where the ¼" seam allowances meet to the edge of the border.

Sew on this line, backstitching to secure the beginning and end of the seam.

If you are happy with the joining, trim off the excess border ¼" and press seam allowance open.

Repeat with other three corners.

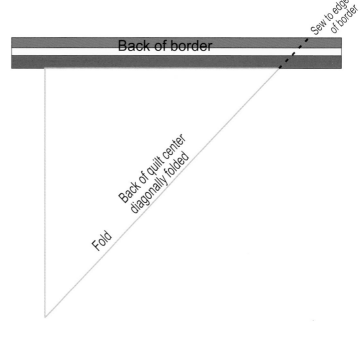

*Merry Christmas*
*to All and to All*
*a Good Night.*

Sue Reich began quilting at her grandmother's farmhouse in northwestern Pennsylvania. Her strong German heritage has provided her with a love of all things Christmas. As a nationally recognized author of quilt history books, Sue travels widely sharing her quilt research and knowledge. Her books include, among many others, *World War I Quilts*; *Quilts Presidential and Patriotic*; and *World War II Quilts*, and she has coauthored books for organizations she has volunteered with, including the Quilts of Valor Foundation.